A Parents' Guide to PANDAS, PANS, and Related Neuroimmune Disorders

A Parents' Guide to PANDAS, PANS, and Related Neuroimmune Disorders

Information, Support, and Advice

Patricia Rice Doran, Christine L. Amabile, Tiffany Tumminaro, Heather Korbmacher, and Diana Pohlman

Jessica Kingsley *Publishers*
London and Philadelphia

First published in 2019
by Jessica Kingsley Publishers
73 Collier Street
London N1 9BE, UK
and
400 Market Street, Suite 400
Philadelphia, PA 19106, USA

www.jkp.com

Library of Congress Cataloging in Publication Data
A CIP catalog record for this book is available from the Library of Congress

British Library Cataloguing in Publication Data
A CIP catalogue record for this book is available from the British Library

ISBN 978 1 78592 768 3
eISBN 978 1 78450 667 4

Printed and bound in the United States

Dedication

Within the community of children (and adults) affected by PANDAS and PANS are many who have fought heroically to overcome significant illness. Among these, some children, adolescents, and young adults have lost their lives. We dedicate this book to Max Wallace and to other children, adolescents, and young adults who have passed away as a result of PANDAS or PANS; their legacy, courage, and perseverance continues to inspire the PANDAS and PANS community.

For more information about the legacy of Max Wallace, please visit: www.salinehealthfoundation.org/pans

Contents

3. Planning, Advocacy, and Communication

Acknowledgements

Unlike many guidebooks on the market, this book represents the collected and hard-won wisdom of a community of parents, children, physicians, nurses and nurse practitioners, counselors and psychologists, educators, and related professionals. In that list, it is not accidental that parents come first, as a great deal of the information captured in this book—even those sections written from a professional perspective—was discovered, vetted, or refined by parents, often with the aid of extraordinary self-awareness and openness on the part of their children. We are grateful, first and foremost, to the community of parents and families affected by PANDAS, PANS, and related disorders. Within that community, it would be remiss not to single out our children (and adults) who have PANDAS and PANS; many times, their willingness to share experiences, try new treatments, and participate in research has paved the way not only for advances in the field but for insights which have made their way into this book.

We are grateful, as well, to many specific individuals and organizations who have generously shared knowledge, reflective feedback, or support. These include Wendy Nawara, whose insight and inspiration were invaluable, the PANDAS Network, and many others. Colleagues at Towson University provided a ready source of encouragement and feedback on current research and practice, as did Dr. Amy Mazur and Ellen Rice, RN, BSN. Claire Doran proved to be a diligent proofreader as the manuscript took shape, and Sabreen Kabir and Anna Melton provided valuable assistance in researching and formatting book elements as well.

Some individuals, while they did not have direct input into this book, nonetheless provided a foundation for us to build upon through their own cutting-edge research or applied scholarship; these include

Dr. Susan Swedo and her colleagues at the National Institutes of Mental Health; the Stanford PANS Clinic physicians and research teams, particularly Dr. Margo Thienemann; Dr. Jamie Candelaria-Greene; and Dr. Janice Tona. Dr. Susan Swedo has dedicated much of her career to researching and advocating for appropriate diagnosis and treatment of PANDAS/PANS and we deeply thank her for her knowledge, compassion, and steadfast dedication to saving our suffering children. The interdisciplinary work of the PANDAS Network Working Group on Educational Access has also inspired some of our collaborative efforts and work in this manuscript. Tim Sorel's documentary *My Kid Is Not Crazy* has focused a much-needed spotlight on the realities of the struggles that face children. His work has validated the efforts of many parents in fighting for their children, and we are beyond grateful for his talent and compassion.

We are particularly grateful to the talented staff at Jessica Kingsley Publishers and Hachette Publishing, who have nurtured this project over the past year, have encouraged us with their patience, and have believed in the value and importance of a comprehensive coping resource for families. In particular, we are appreciative of Rachel Menzies, who first discussed this idea with us, and Sarah Hamlin, whose persistence brought it to completion.

Last but not least, we gratefully acknowledge the love and support of our family members, who have inspired us, shared their own insights about PANDAS and PANS where applicable, and supported us through this collaborative journey. These individuals include: Chad Doran and James, Claire, Katie, Julia, and Conor Doran; Anthony, Lilliana and Ryker Tumminaro; Andrew Amabile (my heart); Donna Leininger (who showed me how to be an amazing mother); Arnold Korbmacher and two tenacious children, Hans and Andre; and once again, the entire PANDAS/PANS community, which in many respects functions for its members as an extended and supportive family.

Preface

As parents affected by PANDAS and PANS, as well as professionals with our own respective spheres of expertise, we have had the opportunity, over the years, to draw upon many sources of high-quality information for families navigating onset, diagnosis, and treatment of this complex disease. In particular, there is an explosion of medical data on this condition within recent years, with over a hundred peer-reviewed articles published within the past five years alone, and these provide excellent resources for parents or professionals desperately seeking to know what treatments offer the greatest likelihood of success for affected patients.

At the same time, we have found, in our own journeys and in our work with other families, that there are few comprehensive resources focused on helping families navigate the significant impact that a PANDAS or PANS diagnosis can have on many areas of day-to-day functioning. Some recent books, such as Dr. Jamie Candelaria-Greene's *PANS, CANS and Automobiles: A Comprehensive Reference for Helping Students with PANDAS and PANS* (2016), and the collaboratively authored *PANDAS and PANS in School Settings: A Handbook for Educators* (Rice Doran 2016), offer practical guidance in navigating non-medical aspects of these conditions, but both are focused to varying degrees on the educational setting and impact on cognition and learning. There are few resources available to help families process, and cope with, the often-devastating impact that PANDAS or PANS can have on family system functioning, individual physical and mental well-being, finances, healthcare coordination, social and community involvement, and multiple other areas. This book is an attempt to meet that need.

This book is divided into several parts. In the first, we address questions and concerns families may have upon initial symptom onset and diagnosis, providing a brief overview of medical research to date and reviewing treatment options and coexisting conditions as well as initial concerns families may have. In the second part, we address strategies and approaches for managing a PANDAS or PANS diagnosis in the long term, recognizing that many families may continue to experience these conditions as chronic illness even when acute symptoms have resolved. In our final part, we address challenges associated with integrating the individual who has PANDAS or PANS back into home and community routines, including school, home, and other venues.

We hope that this book will be helpful to all families whose children (or older loved ones) are encountering this complex set of illnesses. Know that you are not alone and that the PANDAS and PANS community, though you may not have chosen to be part of it, is a passionate and supportive one dedicated to the recovery and success of children.

1

The Physical Realities
of PANDAS and PANS

1

Your Child Has PANDAS or PANS

NOW WHAT?

Driving home from the doctor's office after that first neurology consult, I felt completely overwhelmed. I had surmised Annemarie had PANDAS, of course—that is how we got to the neurologist in the first place. But having a suspicion, and hearing it confirmed starkly by a well-regarded doctor, were two different things and, I was finding out, had two different emotional impacts. My head was spinning thinking of all the steps the doctor had recommended: sterilizing toothbrushes, getting flu reports from the school nurse, starting antibiotics three times a day, restricting playdates with friends who seemed sick or who had sick siblings, monitoring behavior to decide whether and when to initiate steroid therapy, researching child therapists. None of these steps had even been on my radar yesterday, and now they formed part of this scary new reality.

Many parents or caregivers whose children are diagnosed with pediatric autoimmune neuropsychiatric disorders associated with streptococcal infections (PANDAS) or pediatric acute-onset neuropsychiatric syndrome (PANS) may identify with the parent quoted above. A PANDAS or PANS diagnosis can be overwhelming for multiple reasons, and sometimes parents and caregivers need time to adjust to the new status quo.

If your child is newly diagnosed, or if you are continuing to wrap your head around the new reality that PANDAS and PANS have created for your family, this chapter is for you. The chapter begins with a brief overview of each syndrome, based on current medical research. The chapter then briefly addresses common areas of impact, which will be addressed in more detail later in the book. Treatment options, typical progression, and supports are addressed as well, though these are also addressed in greater detail later; in essence, this chapter functions as a quick overview of common issues important for newly diagnosed individuals and their families.

As a parent or caregiver reading this chapter, you may understandably feel overwhelmed at this moment. Indeed, many parents and caregivers report feeling exactly this way. Recent research has found that parents of children with PANS reported a significant "caregiver burden," a term denoting overall stress and emotional response related to providing care (Farmer *et al.* 2018). So first and foremost, know that you are not alone and that stress and trauma are a normal part of patient and family reactions to these complex disorders. Know, too, that treatments are available and that the typical course of PANDAS and PANS, properly treated, does involve improvement.

In fact, there are numerous reasons to be optimistic if your child has received a PANDAS or PANS diagnosis. First and foremost, medical awareness is increasing dramatically. University clinics treating these disorders exist around the U.S., from Massachusetts to California, and clinics or hospitals can be found in other countries, including Australia and those in Europe. For the first time, the ICD-11,[1] the new international diagnostic code manual, used by insurance companies and medical providers, will include a code for PANDAS/PANS, a testimony to the improved awareness of these disorders and their effects. Last, many physicians and psychologists are far more familiar with sudden-onset anxiety and obsessive-compulsive disorder (OCD) symptoms, and their potential autoimmune connection, than in prior years—a development directly related to the continued advocacy of parents as well as the ongoing research of physicians and biologists. So rest assured, while this step in your journey as a parent/caregiver may not have been what you anticipated, there are numerous resources and supports to help you through it—including this book.

---

1   www.who.int/classifications/icd/en

PANDAS and PANS: The fundamentals

We'll begin with a brief history of the disorder. In the early 1990s, the chief pediatric neuroscientist and investigator at the National Institute of Mental Health (NIMH), Dr. Susan Swedo, and her research team were conducting parallel research on pediatric OCD and Sydenham chorea. Members of the team happened to observe that some of the children had an unusually abrupt onset of OCD symptoms. Unlike typical cases of OCD, where symptoms begin gradually and may intensify in the child over a period of several months, the children in this study reported a sudden, dramatic onset and symptoms seemed to escalate in intensity rather quickly. Dr. Swedo described the onset as lightning-like, with the child progressing from mild or no symptoms to debilitating ones in an abrupt amount of time. Most significantly, all of these symptoms were new to the child and a sudden change from their baseline of functioning. The scientists discovered that these new symptoms usually occurred in the aftermath of a strong trigger to the immune system, such as a bacterial strep infection. This disorder was initially named PITANDs (pediatric infection-triggered autoimmune neuropsychiatric disorders). It was shortly renamed PANDAS (pediatric autoimmune neuropsychiatric disorders associated with streptococcal infections), and a study of the first 50 cases was published in 1998 (Swedo *et al.* 1998a). In 2012, the National Institute of Mental Health added the overarching acronym of PANS (pediatric acute-onset neuropsychiatric syndrome), incorporating cases triggered by non-strep and non-infectious agents, which includes PANDAS but also includes obsessive-compulsive and other neuropsychological symptoms triggered by events other than streptococcal infection. These might include, for example, infection with *mycoplasma pneumoniae*, influenza, colds and other viral illnesses, Epstein-Barr virus, and even allergies or metabolic syndromes.

Despite these varying triggers, PANDAS and PANS share common features. Both are marked by an abrupt change, sometimes occurring within hours, in the psychological and/or neurological functioning of those affected. These changes may include sudden onset of obsessive-compulsive symptoms, separation anxiety, or restricted eating, along with additional changes in cognitive functioning, sensory issues, sleep and urinary patterns, motor skills, and emotional or developmental functioning (see Table 1.1 below). While not formally categorized as encephalitis, PANDAS and PANS are frequently linked with, and discussed alongside, post-infectious encephalitic conditions, as they are thought to result from brain inflammation brought on by a "strong stimulant" to the immune system such as illness or allergic reaction (NIMH n.d.).

Table 1.1: Diagnostic criteria for PANDAS/PANS

PANDAS: Diagnostic criteria	PANS: Diagnostic criteria
Presence of OCD and/or tics, particularly multiple, complex, or unusual tics	An abrupt, acute, dramatic onset of obsessive-compulsive disorder or severely restricted food intake
Age requirement (symptoms of the disorder first become evident between three years of age and puberty)	Concurrent presence of additional neuropsychiatric symptoms with similarly severe and acute onset from at least two of the following categories:
Acute onset and episodic (relapsing-remitting) course	• Anxiety
Association with Group A streptococcal (GAS) infection	• Emotional lability and/or depression • Irritability, aggression, and/or severe oppositional behaviors
Association with neurological abnormalities	• Behavioral (developmental) regression
(PANDAS Physicians Network 2018a)	• Sudden deterioration in school performance
	• Motor or sensory abnormalities
	• Somatic signs and symptoms, including sleep disturbances, enuresis, or urinary frequency
	• Symptoms are not better explained by a known neurologic or medical disorder
	• Age requirement—none
	(PANDAS Physicians Network 2018a)

From that point, two decades of research has continued to validate the existence of PANDAS and PANS, with hundreds of peer-reviewed articles appearing in the medical and psychiatric literature.

Diagnostic guidelines

As described by the evaluation guidelines published in 2015, the diagnostic criterion for PANDAS is the abrupt onset of OCD symptoms or tic disorder in pediatric patients (age three years to puberty), where an association is made with Group A streptococcal infection (Chang *et al.* 2015). The child must also have symptoms with an episodic, or relapsing-remitting, course and must demonstrate some neurological abnormalities. The criteria for PANS are an abrupt dramatic onset of

OCD or severely restricted food intake, with concurrent presence of at least two additional acute-onset neuropsychiatric symptoms. Symptoms must not be better explained by another medical disorder; in this sense, PANS is a "diagnosis of exclusion" in that clinicians should exclude other possible explanations or conditions that might produce similar symptoms. The additional neuropsychiatric symptoms include anxiety, emotional lability or depression, behavioral or developmental regression, sudden deterioration in school performance, motor or sensory abnormalities, irritability, aggression or oppositional behaviors, sleep disturbances, and urinary symptoms. The acute onset or severe exacerbation of symptoms is the defining feature in both disorders.

Clinical symptoms

Frequently seen clinical symptoms of PANDAS and PANS include the following:

- Sudden intrusive obsessive thoughts and a need to engage in compulsive, often irrational behaviors. Children with PANDAS or PANS often present with new, dramatic, and disruptive obsessions, or compulsive behaviors. These are sometimes initially missed by parents or caregivers because children may attempt to conceal or minimize them.

- Increased urinary frequency during the day or new onset of bedwetting at night. These urinary symptoms are common among children with PANDAS, though clinicians may initially consider them to be manifestations of a bladder issue, urinary tract infection, or developmental regression.

- Panic or terror stricken, hyperalert facial expression, which may include dilated pupils.

- Neurological abnormalities, including choreiform ("piano-playing") or other odd movements, motor and verbal tics. This may also manifest in handwriting changes and other fine motor impairments.

- Pain in joints, abdomen, or chest, or new-onset headaches. These may also require careful diagnosis and history on the part of clinicians, as they can easily be mistaken for anxiety or other illness.

- Sensory abnormalities or amplifications, where a child may be uncharacteristically and intensely bothered by smells, sounds, tastes, or textures. On occasion, children may hallucinate as well.

- Severe separation anxiety, where a child cannot leave a parent's side or cannot leave a preferred location, such as his or her bedroom. (This symptom often impacts school attendance.)

- Emotional lability or excessive shifts in mood, without an obvious precipitant, or depression, irritability, anger, rages, and oppositional behaviors; generally, an overall abrupt change in personality.

- Developmental regression, such as tantrums, baby talk, or deterioration in functioning of basic skills.

- Eating changes or restrictions, including a new fear of choking or vomiting, fear of contamination or poison, or sensitivity to taste, smell, and texture of food. This symptom is different from anorexia nervosa, though clinicians who are not familiar with PANDAS or PANS may misdiagnose PANS-restricted eating as being symptomatic of anorexia.

- Sleep disruptions occur in many patients, including new onset of nightmares or night terrors, and difficulties falling or staying asleep. Polysomnography sleep studies have demonstrated a variety of abnormalities in children with PANDAS (Gaughan *et al.* 2016).

- Attention and hyperactivity symptoms are frequent in PANDAS children who report new hyperactivity, concentration, and attention difficulties. These children may also demonstrate impairments, deterioration in school performance, and loss of academic abilities, particularly in math and handwriting. Psychological tests of children with PANDAS have found impairments in executive function, dexterity, and on a visual-spatial recall test (Murphy *et al.* 2015).

- A child does not have to have all of these criteria; the presence of only a few can suggest a PANS or PANDAS diagnosis. It has been suggested that this is essentially a spectrum disorder, with some children affected more severely than others. The symptoms, however, are often so profound that most PANDAS families can report an exact date of their child's first experience, often described as the day they lost their child.

Population affected

It is estimated that 1 in 200 children may be affected by PANDAS (Westley 2009). Neuropsychiatric and autoimmune conditions are found to be common among first-degree relatives and siblings of PANDAS patients, possibly suggesting genetic susceptibilities. If you have a child, or work with a child, who is diagnosed with PANDAS or PANS, it is likely that you know at least something about one or both disorders. Survey and informal anecdotal findings from the PANDAS Network, the leading research and advocacy nonprofit, have indicated that many caregivers see multiple physicians before receiving a diagnosis, and many families seek out physicians with experience in PANDAS or PANS after coming across lists of symptoms and wondering for themselves if their child might be affected (PANDAS Network 2018). However, as provider awareness increases, more and more parents and caregivers may be hearing about PANDAS or PANS for the first time at the doctor's office.

Symptoms of PANDAS and PANS may manifest in different ways, which can make diagnosis particularly challenging. The examples in Box 1.1 give some sense of the range and breadth that symptoms can encompass.

Box 1.1: Parents speak about their child's first symptoms

"Our experience with PANDAS was a challenge because our son's onset was very early—he was just four—and very subtle. He began washing his hands over and over and couldn't leave me for a moment without crying. However, he was fine in every other respect, and that first episode resolved on its own after about two weeks—just when I had begun calling child therapists to find an appointment. It wasn't until years later, when he had a formal PANDAS diagnosis, that we put the pieces together and realized his actual onset occurred then."

"My daughter woke up one day a completely different child. She exhibited every symptom listed in the criteria—anxiety, refusal to leave the house, rage, intense OCD. It was as though she was possessed.

The first thing we noticed was this unusual blinking. Over the next few days, it had progressed so my daughter was not just blinking—she was coughing, repeating one or two words constantly, and jerking her head. She had never had tics before, so this was really unusual."

"Our doctor treated my two oldest children but wasn't sure if the third, our daughter who had had immune issues and developmental issues since childhood, had PANDAS or not. She had a lot of anxiety, but didn't have the typical sudden onset or violent episodes that our other children had experienced. I am very grateful our doctor decided to treat her. Two days into antibiotic therapy, her longstanding bedwetting issues disappeared completely. Over time, her anxiety and developmental challenges became much less as well."

Common areas of impact

While symptoms may manifest in ways that vary widely, there are some identified areas which are most frequently affected. These are described below.

Physical

As described in the diagnostic criteria, physical well-being is often affected. Children with PANDAS/PANS may experience sleep disruption, particularly difficulty getting to sleep and staying asleep. They may sleep at odd hours or exhibit narcolepsy—spontaneously falling asleep—throughout the day. They may also have urinary symptoms, such as incontinence or the need to urinate over and over. Anorexia or restricted food intake is also commonly seen in children with PANDAS/PANS.

Emotional and behavioral

One pediatrician has described separation anxiety as a "hallmark symptom" of PANDAS (Kovacevic n.d.), frequently occurring out of the blue or with a dramatic increase in intensity, behavioral symptoms such as anxiety (including fear of leaving home or leaving a preferred person, such as a parent), obsessions, compulsions, rage and aggression, and oppositional behavior. Emotional lability (such as laughing or crying with little notice or without obvious cause) is also not uncommon.

Neurological

All effects of PANDAS, to some extent, are neurological in that they originate with a brain-related syndrome. Several are explicitly and uniquely considered to be neurological symptoms, typically treated with a referral to a neurologist. These include the presence of tics or other motor issues, seizures if present, and attention-deficit hyperactivity disorder (ADHD) symptoms. Motor issues, including fine motor deficits, and sensory sensitivities (sensitivity to light, sound, or touch) can occur.

Box 1.2: Symptoms in focus

Seven-year-old Trixie was a happy-go-lucky child who experienced minor episodes of anxiety that her pediatrician wrote off as "growing pains." However, shortly after recovering from flu, Trixie became very reluctant to leave her room. She developed an unwavering belief that someone had poisoned the family's cereal and refused to eat breakfast unless her mother opened a new cereal box each morning. When prompted to do something she did not feel comfortable doing—such as eating or leaving her bedroom—Trixie, who was rarely aggressive as a rule, would engage in dramatic tantrums. Her parents decided to separate her five-year-old sister, who shared a bedroom ordinarily with Trixie, when Trixie threw a lamp at her little sister's head and narrowly missed smashing her face with it. Trixie's handwriting changed dramatically, and her second-grade teacher called home because she could no longer read anything Trixie wrote. At school, when her parents were able to get her to go, she had difficulty sitting in her seat and her teacher described her as "completely unfocused." Trixie had toilet-trained early as a toddler and never regressed, but she now experienced multiple incidents each day of urinary incontinence.

Treatment progression

Treatment of PANDAS and PANS is covered more fully in subsequent chapters, but a quick summary can be found below.

Treatment often is multi-modal (addressing infection, immune functioning, and behavioral health). The current guidelines for treatment, published by the PANS Consortium in 2017, state that active infection should be treated (Cooperstock *et al.* 2017). Some studies have found a role for prophylaxis with antibiotics and/or anti-inflammatory medication; researchers describe this approach as needing further research, though clinicians report using it widely in practice (Brown *et al.* 2017; Snider *et al.* 2005). Standard psychiatric medicines are sometimes used, generally in lower doses than typically prescribed (Thienemann *et al.* 2017). Cognitive behavioral therapy is recommended for children with PANDAS and PANS, though many parents report, anecdotally, it is most helpful when symptoms have stabilized to the point where a child can successfully and consistently participate in therapy. Immune-modulating therapy is also part of the treatment plan for children with severe illness; this may take the form of steroid medication to reduce inflammation, intravenous immunoglobulin (IVIG—intravenous administration of antibiotics), plasmapheresis (blood cleansing procedure) or powerful immune-modulating drugs such as rituximab (Frankovich *et al.* 2017).

Conclusion and key considerations

It may feel daunting, at the outset, to deal with a diagnosis of PANDAS or PANS. The intensity and complexity of the symptoms, for one, can be challenging for even seasoned physicians. These challenges are intensified, for parents, by the fact that they often occur with little to no warning—so while you and your family are trying to figure out appropriate treatments, therapies, and problem-solving strategies, you are also adjusting to drastic changes in your family life and functioning as well as your child's health. As you consider your initial steps, this book can serve as a guide through many of the challenges associated with PANDAS and PANS— including seeking treatment, ensuring your child's and your own mental health, and navigating life post-recovery. For now, the following steps may be useful:

— *If you have not identified a healthcare provider who is knowledgeable about PANDAS/PANS, encephalitis or related conditions, that is an essential first step.* Several organizations, including PANDAS Network (www.pandasnetwork.org), maintain lists of U.S. and international providers with expertise in treating PANDAS and PANS. Providers are frequently neurologists, immunologists, rheumatologists, or psychiatrists, though general pediatricians, nurse practitioners, and internists may have the required expertise as well.

— *Mental health will be explored more fully in subsequent chapters, but consider, for the present, identifying a counselor, psychologist, or other therapist who can support your child, you, and any other family members.*

— *A helpful initial step is to gather all of your child's medical records in one place so that they are available for easy reference when needed.* You may organize these electronically, using a file storage system, or physically using a binder.

— *If you are not keeping detailed notes of your child's symptoms and response to treatment, you may wish to begin doing so.* Several apps have recently been developed and piloted to assist parents with this task; go to PANDAS Network[2] to find up-to-date information on their availability. As you watch for potential effects of treatment, be patient; parents often report waiting several weeks to see an impact when first beginning treatment, though results can be seen sooner.

---

2   www.pandasnetwork.org

2

What's Happening in Your Child's Brain

The medical context of PANDAS/PANS

This chapter is intended to provide an overview of the current state of knowledge about the medical background of PANDAS and PANS. As you read, please keep in mind that this is designed to be a user-friendly guide to what happens during a PANDAS/PANS episode. Any general information here should not be construed as medical advice; please consult your healthcare provider for any specific questions or guidance. There are several outstanding resources online that provide up-to-date medical information as new research emerges; the PANDAS Physicians Network is primary among these.[1]

History of PANDAS/PANS

There is a lengthy history, in medicine, of infectious disease being linked with psychiatric presentation of illness. Syphilis, for example, manifests with psychiatric symptoms, including psychosis; recent studies have identified increased high-risk behavior in individuals with toxoplasmosis, a parasitic infection transmitted by mice and through cat feces (Flegr 2013). Sydenham chorea, considered a prototype illness for PANDAS, involves obsessive-compulsive symptoms resulting from an autoimmune response to streptococcal infection (PANDAS Network n.d.; Thienemann 2016). More recently, individuals presenting with neurological and psychiatric symptoms have been diagnosed with autoimmune encephalitis (AE), brain inflammation caused by the immune system in response to some stimulant. One of the most famous cases of autoimmune encephalitis in recent years

---

1   www.pandasppn.org

was chronicled by Susannah Cahalan, a *New York Post* reporter whose mysterious illness was eventually diagnosed as anti-NMDA receptor (anti-NMDA-r) encephalitis (Cahalan 2012).

In the mid- to late-1990s, Dr. Susan Swedo, a researcher and developmental pediatrician at the National Institutes of Mental Health, posited a connection between certain cases of obsessive-compulsive disorder in children and concurrent or recent streptococcal infection (Allen, Leonard, and Swedo 1995), with the condition initially termed pediatric infection-triggered autoimmune neuropsychiatric disorders, or PITANDs. Her research eventually led to a paper (Swedo *et al.* 1998) describing a series of 50 patients who exhibited a strange and consistent pattern of symptoms, referred to in the paper as pediatric autoimmune neuropsychiatric disorders associated with streptococcal infections (PANDAS). In addition to demonstrating obsessive-compulsive tendencies, sometimes quite pronounced, these patients demonstrated tics, restricted eating, emotional lability, and changes in fine motor skills and some cognitive skills (such as those needed to do math or write legibly) (Chang *et al.* 2015; Swedo *et al.* 1998). Over time, as further research helped to define characteristic onset, presentation, and symptom course, Swedo's hypothesis became more controversial, leading to a series of papers in which several prominent neurologists discounted or disagreed with her discovery (Kurlan, Johnson and Kaplan 2008).

Nevertheless, research continued, and by 2012 the attention paid to PANDAS, in the scientific community as well as the parent community, had increased. Interested physicians held an expert conference in which they attempted to forge consensus among those who had debated the existence of PANDAS for over a decade in the scientific literature. Out of that conference emerged new terminology, with researchers agreeing on the name pediatric acute-onset neuropsychiatric syndrome (PANS) as a larger category of acute-onset disorders, potentially but not necessarily related to streptococcal infection, resulting in neurological or psychiatric presentation (Swedo, Leckman, and Rose 2012).

Since that time, research has continued into potential factors associated with the onset of PANDAS or PANS and, equally important, potentially successful treatment methods. Over 200 peer-reviewed articles have appeared in print, with studies identifying a role for various illnesses in addition to strep, studies exploring successful treatment methods, and studies further delineating symptoms.

Role of brain regions

PANDAS and PANS have traditionally been hypothesized to affect the basal ganglia region of the brain, which is tied to emotional and motor functions and, in particular, plays a role in one's ability to:

- move appropriately (basal ganglia disorders may involve tremors or fine motor issues)

- feel and respond (basal ganglia disorders may be linked to anxiety, heightened fight or flight reflex, and other emotional difficulties)

- eat and feel hunger, as well as regulating swallowing and chewing

- regulate emotions and sensory responses.

Some research has found anti-basal ganglia antibodies in patients with Sydenham chorea (Church *et al.* 2002; Singer *et al.* 2003), and brain imaging studies have identified swelling in the basal ganglia region for children with PANDAS (Insel 2012). Very recently, research conducted on mice bred to have PANDAS-like symptoms and illness found that inflammation occurs not only in the basal ganglia region but also in other areas of the brain, such as the amygdala, which involves sensations of fear and the fight or flight reflex (Platt, Agalliu, and Cutforth 2017). Such studies demonstrate the role of inflammation in the sudden onset of symptoms seen with PANDAS and PANS. It's hypothesized (and, increasingly, demonstrated by peer-reviewed studies) that such inflammation is caused by an aberrant immune response. Within the past few years, researchers have identified potential biomarkers in blood for inflammation (Moleculera Labs 2018) in the brain. The researchers involved in this work have formed a company, Moleculera Laboratories, which specializes in measuring the levels of anti-basal ganglia antibodies in the blood. This test, referred to as the Cunningham Panel (after its creator, Dr. Madeline Cunningham), is sometimes used by physicians as part of the diagnostic process.

Encephalitis and brain inflammation

In recent years, new advances have occurred connecting psychiatric symptoms to encephalitis, also classified as swelling or inflammation of brain tissue, particularly autoimmune encephalitis. The bestselling book *Brain on Fire*, mentioned above, describes the *New York Post* reporter's episode of autoimmune encephalitis, initially presenting with psychiatric symptoms, and her subsequent recovery (Cahalan 2012). New awareness has led to increased understanding and more frequent diagnoses for conditions such as anti-NMDA receptor encephalitis and has also identified other forms of autoimmune encephalitis that may have previously unrecognized triggers (Dalmau and Graus 2018).

Encephalitis has long been considered a serious and rare disease of the brain, resulting in brain inflammation from any one of several sources. While PANDAS and PANS are not currently classified, formally, as encephalitic disorders, numerous researchers and clinicians have pointed out areas of commonality in the pathology of both disorders (Najjar *et al.* 2013; Platt, Agalliu, and Cutforth 2017).

Common symptoms

As described in the diagnostic criteria, common symptoms of PANDAS and PANS often overlap, even if the trigger for each syndrome may differ for individual patients and in the research literature. Parents and caregivers often report noticing changes in children's (or adults', in some cases) overall functioning, particularly in areas of behavior and psychological functioning (including obsessive-compulsive symptoms, increased attention and focus difficulties, and sometimes rage and aggression). For many children, a new, overwhelming and sudden separation anxiety is notable; children who previously went to school, daycare or friends' homes without difficulty suddenly will not leave their parent's side or the safety of their bedroom.

Sleep patterns are often disrupted; children may experience difficulty getting to sleep, may experience excessive drowsiness or even narcolepsy, or may wake multiple times throughout the night. Urinary symptoms may occur, including frequent urination, compulsive use of the bathroom, a sensation of feeling as though one needs to urinate constantly, and sometimes urinary or bowel incontinence. In very young children, it may be difficult to distinguish these symptoms from the ups and downs of typical toilet training, and parents may find it helpful to consider whether recurrence or new occurrence of urinary symptoms has occurred in conjunction with any other symptoms. Motor symptoms may also occur, including gross motor difficulties, tics or involuntary movements, and new difficulties with fine motor functioning. Sometimes parents may report this as increased clumsiness or changes in handwriting. Changes in eating patterns are also characteristic of children with PANDAS and PANS; these may include new-onset anorexia or restricted eating, fear of contamination or aversion to specific foods, difficulty swallowing or fear of choking. Sometimes, children may go to some lengths to hide changes in food consumption from parents, and changes in eating habits may present with uneaten school lunches coming home, stomach pain, or with a sudden plateau or plunge on a growth chart. Children may also experience general somatic symptoms, including generalized headache or stomach ache symptoms.

Treatment options

Treatment options are discussed more fully in Chapter 4, which summarizes recent peer-reviewed treatment guidelines disseminated by a consortium of leading physicians across several countries. In brief, treatment often focuses on quelling inflammation in order to facilitate healing, treating, and eradicating any underlying infection (such as streptococcal infection or chronic mycoplasma) using antibiotics, antivirals and other approaches to combat infection, and treating the immune system dysfunction that leads to inflammation (Chang *et al.* 2015; Cooperstock *et al.* 2017; Frankovich *et al.* 2017; Thienemann *et al.* 2017). There is also a widely acknowledged role for psychological and psychiatric therapies to alleviate symptoms of obsessive-compulsive disorder (OCD) (Thienemann *et al.* 2017).

Conclusion and key considerations

Medical research in this area is rapidly evolving, and even within the last five years new guidelines for treatment have been established. The underlying dysfunction that leads to brain inflammation and changes in neurological or psychological functioning must be addressed on a variety of levels, with multiple treatments, and sometimes with the aid of multiple physicians. As a parent, you may find this process overwhelming; at this stage, as you contemplate your child's initial diagnosis and formulate an initial treatment plan, the following may be helpful:

> — *Seek second opinions when necessary.* Because PANDAS and PANS are not frequently diagnosed and were identified relatively recently, they may

not have been addressed in your primary care provider's initial training or recent professional development. Many primary care physicians may be unaware of the patterns of symptom presentation or may apply more stringent diagnostic criteria than those accepted by peer-reviewed guidelines. We have encountered, for example, physicians who refuse to make a diagnosis of PANDAS or PANS without positive results on blood tests for recent or current strep infection (also known as "strep titers") or presentation of tics—neither of which practices is consistent with peer-reviewed diagnostic guidelines.

— *Maintain documentation and accurate histories.* Medical offices may switch between electronic and paper-based medical records, may fail to send records due to oversight or administrative error, and may send incomplete records when you assume they are sending complete ones. For these reasons, you will want to maintain your own copies of your child's medical records, including notes from tests, procedures, and office visits. Maintain records from general practitioners and specialists, and plan to bring these to new-patient appointments with new providers. Do not rely on each physician's (or other provider's) office to resend documents for each new appointment; among other reasons, you'll find yourself racking up significant copying fees from practices that charge them! Rather, maintain your own complete and up-to-date copy of your child's records, and hand-carry them to each appointment.

— *Create an organizational system for medical information.* A hard-copy binder, as well as regularly updated electronic files, can help you keep all of your information organized—especially as the amount of information you have will increase rapidly if you end up needing to see multiple specialists or seek second or third opinions. In your filing system, include a document that, to the best of your ability, summarizes your child's timeline in terms of initial triggers, onset of illness, and subsequent exacerbation or flares. This will be helpful to new providers in offering a quick, easy to grasp overview of your child's history and current status.

3

Complex Cases and Comorbid Conditions

Marissa was diagnosed with PANDAS at age seven and responded well to high-dose antibiotic and steroid therapy. Her symptoms, which included restricted eating, rage, aggression, illegible handwriting and academic challenges at school, and separation anxiety, diminished significantly; her father (who was her primary caregiver) rated her symptom intensity as a 9 out of 10 upon diagnosis and a 2 out of 10 after treatment. Her neurologist at first recommended IVIG but then changed her treatment plan upon her rapid improvement, feeling that less invasive therapies might be most appropriate. A year and a half later, Marissa's PANDAS symptoms had virtually resolved. However, she still complained almost daily of headaches, stomach aches, and dizziness. Marissa's father returned to her treating PANDAS physician, who advised the family to see a cardiologist to be screened for postural orthostatic tachycardia syndrome (POTS) as well as seeing an immunologist to rectify an underlying immune deficiency.

Like Marissa's family, many parents and children dealing with PANDAS and PANS find that their initial diagnosis may provide them some answers but may not conclusively address all aspects of their child's health. Indeed, children with PANDAS and PANS often have a more complicated medical journey than many of their peers. In fact, while research is ongoing, some surveys report that parents of children with PANDAS and PANS often have seen multiple doctors and received multiple diagnoses prior to getting their PANDAS or PANS diagnosis (Calaprice, Tona, and Murphy 2017a). These findings reflect the complexity of dealing with PANDAS and PANS in terms of both diagnosis and treatment; some parents compare the treatment process to peeling back layers of an onion. The complexities of treatment can be intensified by difficulty in obtaining an accurate diagnosis as well as challenges in treating comorbid (or co-occurring) conditions alongside PANDAS or PANS.

Diagnosis: Complexities of seeking diagnosis

The process of seeking and receiving a diagnosis is often complicated by symptoms which present in ways that meet criteria for multiple disorders. For example, sudden-onset eating restrictions may be mistaken for traditional presentations of anorexia nervosa or body dysmorphia disorder, particularly if the physician has not taken the time to gather a complete history. Sudden-onset tics or motor difficulties may mimic a more classic presentation of Tourette's syndrome (Harris 2014). Physicians who are not familiar with the varied presentations of PANDAS or PANS may have difficulty identifying either syndrome if the presentation is complex or subtle or if a child has been ill for some time, making the "sudden-onset" (NIMH n.d.) aspect more difficult to detect.

Parents and caregivers may find it challenging to find a physician who has experience with PANDAS and PANS, often necessitating out-of-state travel, upfront payment for providers who do not take insurance, and other logistical hurdles. A majority of parents in a recent PANDAS Network survey indicated seeing more than three providers prior to receiving the correct diagnosis, with some seeing six or more (PANDAS Network 2018). As parents seeking diagnosis, particularly for a child whose symptom presentation is complex, you may find yourself devoting substantial time and financial resources to the process, increasing stress on yourself, your partner, and your other children as well as the child with PANDAS or PANS. Keep in mind the self-help resources that we discuss later in this book.

As a reminder, this book is written by professionals in varying fields, including social work, cognitive behavioral therapy, family outreach, and special education. However, we do not presume to give medical advice here, and our perspective on complex medical cases, as well as comorbid conditions, is that of experienced parents and non-medical practitioners. Always seek advice and information on your child's health from your child's healthcare team, including both physical and mental or behavioral health providers.

Treatment: Complexities of treating

As parents, particularly if your child is newly diagnosed, bear in mind that your management strategies for a child with severe, life-threatening illness will necessarily be different from those that apply to children with mild or moderate illness. In particular, much of the guidance around school and social functioning may be irrelevant if your child is currently unable to attend school, currently housed in a psychiatric institution or long-term care facility, or unable to safely be around others.

Each of these situations may be unique. However, the following general principles may be helpful to keep in mind in any challenging or complex situation—whatever coexisting condition might be involved (see the discussion at the end of this chapter for specific examples of additional illnesses or conditions). See also Chapters 5 and 8 for more specific suggestions about managing crisis situations, particularly in the realm of behavior.

- *Your first priority is your child's safety and survival.* As discussed below, dealing with severe or complex cases of PANS requires families to prioritize. Your child's survival is likely more important than anything else affecting your family—jobs, school, team experiences. It is challenging to balance the needs of a severely ill child against those of healthy siblings whose emotional well-being may be at stake, but do bear in mind that PANDAS and PANS can be serious, even life-threatening illnesses when families do not have prompt access to treatment. While states of crisis are draining and debilitating for all family members, they are not permanent—once you reach a point of stability, you can begin to explore other options to allow you and other family members to resume your daily living activities.

- *If at all possible, ensure that your medical team includes a provider with experience of treating severe—not just moderate or mild—cases of PANDAS or PANS.* Some families report making one or two trips a year to a provider who sees children with significant illness, coordinating the remaining care visits with a local, less experienced physician who nevertheless can call on the more experienced practitioner when needed. From our experience, we strongly recommend this step for families dealing with severe symptom presentation, as input from an experienced professional may make a significant difference in the treatment process.

- *It is likely that you'll need to triage problems, priorities, and goals.* If your child is currently suicidal, for example, you may change his school or sports schedule to ensure that you are able to provide him with round-the-clock supervision. Similarly, if your child is in an acute crisis regarding food restriction, school attendance may be less important, even if it means that she will eventually need to repeat a year of high school.

- *To the best of your ability, prioritize self-care as well.* This is, of course, easier said than done; when your child is in crisis, and you are shuttling back and forth between your other children and an inpatient neurology or psychiatric unit, there are likely no opportunities to sneak away for a massage or lunch date. Consider asking friends for assistance so that you are able to see a therapist if necessary, take a nap, or take a walk outside. If possible, check with the social work office at your child's hospital or medical center to see if they can suggest respite care or other resources. If making this contact is beyond your capacity at the moment, ask a trusted family member or friend to contact them on your behalf and relay any recommendations to you. Prioritizing self-care also, in many cases, means letting go of guilt regarding whatever you have not been able to do. Your other children may miss sports tournaments or birthday parties; you may forget your spouse or partner's birthday; you may be less attentive or emotionally available to your other loved ones than you would like. Disappointing and upsetting as they may be in the short term, these effects will not last forever. If you are finding that you need to let other things go in the short term while you support your child with PANDAS or PANS, that is not a cause for guilt—rather, it is a cause to acknowledge that you are doing your best and, likely, attending to your most important responsibility at the moment. Keep in mind that a recent study found that caregiver burden, for parents of children with PANS, can be higher than that of parents whose children have pediatric cancer (Thienemann 2017), and parents frequently report extreme stress associated with the diagnosis and treatment process—so while that situation is not ideal, you are in good company if you feel this way too.

Comorbid (or co-occurring) conditions

While this book is not intended to serve as medical advice, it does draw upon reported experiences of parents and reports found in the medical literature. Anecdotally, many parents report having children with multiple diagnoses, such as PANDAS, autism spectrum disorders, generalized anxiety disorder, allergic rhinitis, and the like. A few of these commonly co-occurring conditions are discussed here. While advice on medical management is outside the scope of this book, as discussed above, some suggestions for navigating the medical system and communicating with practitioners are provided.

Anxiety

Anxiety is a commonly reported symptom of PANDAS and PANS, and some parents report it as one of the first to appear. More specific suggestions for managing psychiatric and behavioral symptoms appear in Part 2 of this book. However, at the initial diagnosis phase, you will want to make sure that any provider treating anxiety symptoms is also familiar with the relevant background information on PANDAS and PANS. It is important, for example, that counselors, psychologists, psychiatrists, or social workers dealing with PANDAS-induced (or PANS-induced) anxiety are familiar with some of the potential triggers for each condition (see Box 3.1, which provides a list of questions to ask a provider, for some guidance in selecting a PANDAS or PANS-friendly provider for PANDAS or PANS, or for any comorbid condition).

Autism spectrum disorders

Recent studies have identified potential overlap between autism spectrum disorders and PANDAS in terms of symptom presentation, laboratory results, and biomarkers (Connery et al. 2018). Some children with autism spectrum disorders, like those with PANDAS or other immune dysfunction, report improvement with IVIG treatment (Connery et al. 2018), suggesting potential immunological aspects to both disorders. Anecdotally, we know multiple parents who first considered an autism spectrum diagnosis for their child, as symptom presentation for PANDAS often includes sensory, motor, and communication challenges similar to those seen in autism spectrum challenges. In distinguishing between the two, we cannot emphasize strongly enough the value of seeing a practitioner who is knowledgeable and well versed in both conditions. It is also not uncommon, in our anecdotal experience, for children to be dually diagnosed: to receive a diagnosis of autism spectrum disorder and then, after family members learn about PANDAS or PANS, to receive that diagnosis as well, or to receive a diagnosis of underlying autism spectrum disorder with additional exacerbation due to PANDAS or PANS.

Orthostatic disorders and dysautonomia

As in the vignette at the beginning of this chapter, there is a substantial minority of children and adults in the PANDAS/PANS community who seem to experience disorders of the autonomic nervous system, such as postural orthostatic tachycardia syndrome (POTS) or orthostatic intolerance (OI), conditions commonly associated with fainting, fatigue, lightheadedness, dizziness, and headaches (Garland, Celedonio, and Raj 2015). These conditions are thought to have an autoimmune basis in some cases as well (Garland *et al.* 2015), given that they have been sometimes found to respond to IVIG and antibiotic treatment (Weinstock *et al.* 2018). While research into this comorbidity is scarce thus far, informal PANDAS or PANS support groups are excellent places to find information from other families who may be navigating similar conditions, as well as about referrals to practitioners who are knowledgeable about both conditions. Diagnosis can be challenging for individuals affected by both PANDAS/PANS and POTS, OI, or other autonomic disorders, as both may present with some similar symptoms (headaches, stomach aches, anxiety, fatigue). Treatment of POTS or OI symptoms, or avoidance of triggers, sometimes brings relief. However, some individuals with POTS or OI have more significant illness and may need intensive medical treatment as well. As with mental health providers, we recommend explicitly seeking out a provider who is familiar with both PANDAS/PANS and POTS/OI.

Immune deficiency

Some children who have PANDAS or PANS report receiving treatment for coexisting immune deficiency, and immune system issues in general are reported to occur at an increased rate among individuals with autoimmunity (Cunningham-Rundles 2011). Immune deficiency can be particularly problematic in children with PANDAS or PANS as it may predispose them to illness, which perpetuates recurrence of symptoms. Some families treat mild immune deficiency with lifestyle modifications such as healthy diets and reduced exposure to illness. Others may treat with immunoglobulin therapy, often in lowered doses, to build up their child's immunity. Low-dose IVIG, a standard treatment for documented immune deficiency, has been anecdotally reported by parents to benefit some children with PANDAS or PANS once acute infections and symptoms are resolved and long-term immune support can be considered; however, the guidance of a PANDAS or PANS specialist is critical in determining when lower doses for immune deficiency, as opposed to the higher doses used to treat autoimmunity, may be appropriate.

Other autoimmune disorders

Medical knowledge in this area is growing rapidly. Children with PANDAS-like symptoms are at increased likelihood of autoimmune issues in their family history (Calaprice *et al.* 2017b). Some families elect to see rheumatologists for autoimmune issues, who may also be well positioned to address their child's PANDAS or PANS. While treatments for PANDAS or PANS may overlap with treatments for other autoimmune disorders, such as rituximab or IVIG (Frankovich *et al.* 2017), separate treatments may be required before, alongside, or after primary PANDAS or PANS treatments. In any event, if children have preexisting autoimmune conditions, it is wise to be vigilant about avoiding potential triggers. In addition, it may be useful to ensure that all members of the PANDAS or PANS treatment team (including therapist, psychiatrist, nutritionist, etc.) have a working knowledge of autoimmune issues, including any potential overlap between autoimmune conditions and neuropsychiatric symptoms.

Allergies and allergic disorders

One parent quoted in a recent book recounted her son's allergies as being so severe that mowing the grass caused his PANDAS symptoms to flare (Rice Doran 2016). As PANS may be triggered by any immune system stimulant (Chang *et al.* 2015), children who have severe allergies may need additional attention throughout treatment to guard against relapses. Having an allergist or immunologist, along with a treating PANDAS specialist (unless your treating PANS specialist is an immunologist), may be helpful and is a topic to discuss with your PANDAS or PANS specialist.

Digestive issues and food intolerance

Stomach pain is reported frequently by children with PANDAS or PANS (Chang *et al.* 2015) and can be a symptom of strep or other viral or bacterial infection. For this reason, parents should have a sympathetic, well-informed general healthcare provider who can assist in differentiating infectious and other sources of stomach pain. In addition, parents who find that their child has underlying digestive issues (such as celiac disease, leaky gut syndrome, or intolerance that may not rise to the level of allergy) should consult with appropriate specialists as needed. As with some other aspects of illness, providers should be mindful of the ways in which restricted diets may impact PANDAS symptoms. A child with restricted eating behaviors, for example, may experience difficulty adhering to a strict gluten-free diet and maintaining adequate calorie intake; consultation with an experienced physician, along with specialists such as nutritionists and gastroenterologists, may be needed.

Generalized fine motor impairments and sensory processing challenges

Fine motor challenges are a recognized symptom of PANDAS and PANS (Chang *et al.* 2015), and these may cause difficulties for children independent of other PANDAS or PANS symptoms. Similarly, children diagnosed with PANDAS or PANS may experience sensory sensitivities and sensory processing challenges; some parents in our experience have reported these as the first PANDAS symptoms to appear. Occupational therapists are critical members of care teams, both in the medical context for patient care and in school or other clinical settings, as they can consult on technology to support handwriting, productive approaches to therapy, and postural or other environmental supports for both fine motor and sensory issues. Numerous articles and books in recent years have addressed the role of occupational therapy in treatment plans for children with these disorders (Calaprice *et al.* 2017a, 2017b).

Attention-deficit hyperactivity disorder (ADHD) and executive function challenges

ADHD and executive function difficulties may appear as part of overall symptom presentation for children with PANDAS or PANS, either concurrently with other symptoms or in sequence. (Executive function refers to a set of interrelated cognitive skills, broadly related to working memory, inhibiting responses, and cognitive flexibility or being able to adapt to shifts in circumstances (The Understood Team n.d.) Additionally, some research has found that difficulties with attention and executive function may persist even years after the resolution of other symptoms in post-infectious encephalitis (Pawela *et al.* 2017). Comprehensive neuropsychological evaluation is recommended for any children with prior PANDAS or PANS diagnoses who continue to exhibit difficulties in either of these areas, as they may benefit from academic or behavioral accommodations even after other PANDAS or PANS symptoms have resolved.

Lyme disease

A comprehensive discussion of tick-borne illnesses is well beyond the scope of this book, unfortunately. Lyme disease and other tick-borne illnesses are well known for having significant neurological, psychological, and physical impact in both the short and long term, as well as impact on healthcare costs and quality of life (Adrion *et al.* 2015; Davidsson 2018; Khakpour 2018). Lyme disease and related co-infections (such as babesia and bartonella) can continue to impact the immune system, particularly if the original bacterial infection is difficult to clear. Many families in our experience end up working with both a PANDAS or PANS specialist and, additionally, a Lyme or tick-borne illness specialist, drawing on the expertise of both physicians to manage both autoimmune neuropsychiatric effects and the effects of the original illness. Families may consider seeing a Lyme or tick-borne illness specialist when their child receives a positive test for Lyme disease or tick-borne illness, when their child displays symptoms consistent with tick-borne illness (such as joint pain or the characteristic bulls-eye rash associated with Lyme disease), or when PANDAS or PANS symptoms fail to resolve as expected, suggesting additional undiagnosed issues.

Box 3.1: Questions to ask your provider

As you select a provider, consider asking the following questions to determine their familiarity with PANDAS and PANS and their experience base in treating mild, moderate, and significant presentations of each disorder and their knowledge base in treating comorbid conditions linked to PANDAS or PANS.

- Have you treated many children or adults with PANDAS and PANS? If so, can you share how many?

- Have you treated many children or adults whose symptoms related to [whatever relevant disorder is involved] also involved PANDAS or PANS symptoms?

- Were most of these children mild, moderate, or severe in their presentation?

- What therapies or approaches have you found to be most useful for your patients with PANDAS or PANS/your patients with [whatever relevant disorder is involved]?

- Have you seen significant interplay or relationship between PANDAS and PANS and [whatever relevant disorder is involved]? If so, does that impact your approach to treatment, and how so?

- How do you decide which therapies to use?

- Have you been able to attend any recent conferences or continuing medical education (CME) events on PANDAS or PANS? Have you been able to read any of the current [within the last two years] peer-reviewed articles or research summaries on these disorders?

- Can you share how long your patients with PANDAS or PANS typically take to recover? If it varies, what factors do you think are most relevant in determining the timeframe for recovery? Does this differ from your patients without PANDAS or PANS?

- Are you willing to communicate directly with insurance companies if there are disputes about coverage resolution? Have you had difficulties with coverage for various treatments?

- How do you recommend patients and families handle relapse and exposure to illness after diagnosis?

Conclusion and key considerations

Both PANDAS and PANS may occur in conjunction with other disorders, and children with either disorder may have prior diagnoses or comorbid conditions. Assembling a healthcare team with knowledgeable specialists, for all relevant conditions, is critical. The following suggestions may be helpful as parents and caregivers navigate the complexities of multiple diagnoses and conditions:

— *Continue seeking answers.* If your child's symptoms do not resolve as expected upon treatment by a knowledgeable PANDAS or PANS specialist (a process which, as your physician can tell you, may take time) be prepared to consider the possibility of additional comorbid illnesses. Often, PANDAS or PANS specialists are familiar with a range of additional diagnoses and can refer you to the appropriate provider, or request initial testing, to investigate other diagnoses.

— *Ensure all members of your child's care and educational teams are familiar with relevant diagnoses.* Sometimes, educating school personnel about PANDAS or PANS can be a significant task in itself, and it may seem overwhelming to also explain POTS or Lyme disease and ask school staff to accommodate for those conditions as well. Rest assured, federal disability and anti-discrimination laws, in most cases, are designed to ensure your child is protected regardless of the nature or number of diagnoses at play. For example, your child may receive academic accommodations for PANDAS and may also receive health-related accommodations (such as a shortened day or additional water breaks) for POTS. You may find that, while your child's accommodations for PANDAS or PANS can be modified for non-symptomatic periods, it is necessary to keep accommodations in place year-round for other more consistently symptomatic conditions.

— *Educate yourself, your child, and others about the interplay between related conditions.* ADHD symptoms may be present all the time but may worsen during PANDAS exacerbations; underlying Lyme disease may cause PANS symptoms to worsen at certain times. Communicating this to school personnel, medical providers, and coaches or counselors may require multiple conversations in which you provide supporting documentation and educational material. You may find the following nonprofits and educational or advocacy organizations to be particularly useful sources for educational material (note that listing an organization here does not imply our endorsement of any or all specific content on their website).

American Occupational Therapy Association: www.aota.org

Autism Society of America: www.autism-society.org

Autism Speaks: www.autismspeaks.org

Child Mind Institute: (for sensory, fine motor, ADHD/executive function, and anxiety): https://childmind.org

Dysautonomia International: www.dysautonomiainternational.org

ILADS (International Lyme and Associated Diseases Society): www.ilads.org

Lyme Disease Association: www.lymediseaseassociation.org

LymeDisease.org: www.lymedisease.org

National Autism Association: http://nationalautismassociation.org

National Center for Learning Disabilities: resource site (for ADHD and executive function issues): www.understood.org

4

Common Treatments and Therapies for PANDAS/PANS

Overview

This chapter aims to provide an overview of the current state of medical and behavioral therapies for PANDAS, PANS, and related conditions, including encephalitic syndromes (though encephalitis is classified currently as a different disorder and is not a primary focus of this chapter). In providing this information, we must first note that medical discoveries in this area are progressing rapidly, and it is likely that between the time we write this chapter and the time it is printed, new research will be published and new treatment paradigms will emerge. Therefore, we strongly recommend that readers supplement this chapter with some of the current online resources highlighted in Box 4.1; these websites typically have the most current research and treatment guidelines posted.

Box 4.1: Recommended sources of up-to-date medical information

As with many newly identified syndromes, the research on PANDAS and PANS changes rapidly. These organizations and sites are typically updated frequently and thus are reliable sources of information.

PANDAS Network: http://pandasnetwork.org

NIMH (National Institute of Mental Health): www.nimh.nih.gov/labs-at-nimh/research-areas/clinics-and-labs/sbp/information-about-pans-pandas.shtml

PPN (PANDAS Physicians Network): www.pandasppn.org

Current treatment guidelines

In 2017 the PANS Research Consortium published treatment guidelines refining recommendations that represent best practices from knowledgeable experts, researchers, and treatment providers from across the U.S. (Cooperstock *et al.* 2017; Frankovich *et al.* 2017; Thienemann *et al.* 2017). These recommendations highlight the key points of identifying and eradicating the underlying infection, calming the ramped-up immune reaction and resulting brain inflammation. Treatment has a three-tiered approach:

1. Treat the psychiatric and behavioral symptoms with psychotherapy and behavioral interventions and psychiatric medications (if needed) (Thienemann *et al.* 2017).

2. Treat the source of infection with select antibiotics (Cooperstock *et al.* 2017).

3. Treat the immune system with immune-modulatory and anti-inflammatory treatments (Frankovich *et al.* 2017).

Guidelines also suggest that clinicians prioritize treatment of symptoms causing the greatest distress and interference, and tailor therapies on the basis of symptom severity and disease trajectory. Since symptom presentations differ, therapies should be individualized and tailored to meet each child's specific needs. The PANDAS Physician Network has recommendations based on the level of symptom severity, including mild, moderate, severe, and chronic state. An initial course of antibiotics often is recommended for newly diagnosed children with PANDAS, including those who may not test positive for infection but whose history is suggestive of exposure to infection. Many clinicians find with new-onset symptoms that a longer-term course (20 to 30 days) of antibiotics may be effective; if illness is more entrenched, a longer course of antibiotics may be needed. If diagnosed early, research suggests that patients may experience significant improvement in symptoms with just antibiotic treatment, and improvements may be visible within a few weeks (PANDAS Physicians Network 2018a). Parents are encouraged to have their facts ready prior to meeting with their child's doctor and to provide any and all supporting documentation or recommendations, particularly for physicians who are not familiar with use of antibiotics to treat PANDAS symptoms.

Follow-up laboratory testing may be recommended to confirm that the initial infection is gone. Treatment may be necessary in the future, if the child is exposed again to strep and symptoms return. A physician may also recommend immune modulators such as steroids or non-steroidal anti-inflammatory medications (NSAIDs) or antihistamines such as Benadryl. Steroids may temporarily exacerbate aggression and mania-like symptoms, but a positive response is a good indication that further immunomodulation therapy could be helpful if indicated. For psychiatric symptoms, cognitive behavioral therapy (CBT) can be started with the child as soon as they can tolerate it and in the interim with parents for education and support. Psychiatric medications can be used with caution but are often prescribed in lower doses than for children with non-PANDAS psychiatric symptoms (PANDAS Physicians Network 2018b).

If PANDAS is not diagnosed quickly and symptoms continue, more aggressive treatments may be needed. Intravenous immunoglobulin (IVIG) is a treatment whereby the child receives intravenous administration of antibodies pooled from thousands of donors. Plasmapheresis (sometimes abbreviated to PEX, for plasma exchange) is a blood cleaning procedure involving the removal, treatment, and return of plasma to remove antibodies through a surgically placed port catheter. The PANDAS Physicians Network has provided protocols for administration of both these therapies (see PANDAS Physicians Network 2018c). However, both of these procedures include risks, as well as being expensive and often not covered by insurance. If PANDAS symptoms fail to improve after intensive interventions, consideration should be given to the possibility that therapeutic efforts are best redirected toward rehabilitation and supportive therapies. Autoimmune diseases are extremely difficult to treat and even with these aggressive interventions, doctors are not always successful.

At this time, it is not always possible to predict the progression or long-term course of illness in PANDAS (Chang *et al.* 2015). Many children will recover after an extended-length dose of antibiotics. Others have subsequent symptom relapses or flares after periods of remission (particularly if they are exposed again to infections), while some children develop a chronic autoimmune condition that requires ongoing and more intensive treatment. We do know that delays in diagnosis and treatment often result in increased chronic symptoms.

Research suggests that those who have achieved complete resolution of the initial inciting infection with early and aggressive antibiotics were significantly more likely to completely return to pre-episode state and significantly less likely to experience residual symptoms or recurrences in the future (Chang *et al.* 2015). Thus, the importance of early identification and treatment is paramount.

Multidisciplinary treatment approach

Cross-disciplinary collaboration is most successful for treatment, and each profession can offer key contributions. Medical providers such as pediatricians, immunologists, neurologists, rheumatologists, infectious disease physicians, as well as mental health providers such as psychiatrists, psychologists, and therapists, can play a valuable role in diagnosis and treatment, particularly when they establish a team approach. In the school, this team can consist of a special education team—nurse, counselors, social workers, and psychologists— for support. With PANDAS, the parent is often the driving force, desperately seeking to get back their normal functioning child. It is key to find providers who will support and collaborate with the family, as the majority of parents are traumatized and greatly need compassion.

Box 4.2: Questions to ask a potential mental healthcare provider

- My child has PANDAS/PANS. Are you familiar with these conditions? What do you know about them?

- How many children or adults with PANDAS or PANS have you treated? Can you share about your general approach to treatment for this population?

- How might your approach or delivery differ for a patient with PANDAS and PANS as opposed to a patient with uncomplicated anxiety or OCD?

- Do you have experience with mild, moderate, or severe forms of PANDAS or PANS, or all of the above?

- My child is currently stable enough to participate in therapy. If my child were to experience a significant relapse, what are your thoughts about whether, when, and how to continue with therapy?

Nutrition and complementary approaches

In addition to these medical treatments which address infection, many parents have reported benefits in alternative interventions, including supplements and diet changes. Probiotics may support gut flora and help modulate immune reactions and susceptibility to infection. Vitamin D as well as Omega 3 supplements have been shown to be beneficial to immune support as well.

Some parents, anecdotally, report having seen improvement with dietary adjustments such as adoption of gluten-free, dairy-free, or organic diets. Anti-inflammatory diets emphasizing whole foods, few processed foods, and fruits and vegetables are popular. For children who find specific foods provoke allergic reactions, avoiding those foods may help to minimize symptoms.

Parents also report that, in addition to minimizing PANDAS and PANS symptoms, following healthy eating guidelines can improve children's overall health by minimizing illness and increasing their ability to fight off infections. Supplementing with vitamin C supplements or fruits high in vitamin C, for example, has been reported by some parents to be helpful during winter months when exposure to infections may be more common.

See Box 4.3 for a sample daily menu for a child using an anti-inflammatory diet.

Box 4.3: Sample anti-inflammatory menu

Breakfast: Fresh fruit; yogurt or smoothie (including dairy-free smoothies); eggs or, if allergic, another protein source

Snack: Apple or clementine slices, fresh berries, fresh vegetables with hummus; gluten-free muffin; nuts or edamame if not allergic

Lunch: Non-processed meat (chicken breast, organic sliced turkey, etc.); salad, vegetables, and/or quinoa; (gluten-free) pita bread

Snack: Sunflower butter on celery; gluten-free crackers with cheese (dairy-free or dairy); fresh fruit

Dinner: Meat; vegetables or salad; whole grains (brown rice, quinoa, couscous blend); gluten-free/dairy-free dessert as indicated

Beyond nutrition, it is important to consider the potential impact of restricted eating behaviors and OCD-related concerns when planning menus. Cassandra, a nine-year-old with patterns of restricted eating related to contamination OCD and avoidance of meat products, also tested positive for gluten and dairy sensitivities. In consultation with her pediatrician and PANDAS neurologist, Cassandra's parents decided to allow her to continue to include gluten and dairy in her diet until her obsessive-compulsive issues improved.

There also appears to be some benefit in reducing stress, which is thought to weaken the blood-brain barrier, though research in this area is still developing (Lehmann *et al.* 2018). Reducing stress to all family members, particularly the child diagnosed with PANDAS or PANS, may be challenging and the assistance of a professional counselor or therapist can be invaluable here. Reducing exposure to illness, particularly for newly diagnosed individuals, is also critical in preventing worsening of symptoms or relapse post-recovery. Strategies for preventing and reducing exposure, particularly in school settings, are reviewed in Chapter 16.

Conclusion and key considerations

Research on best practices for treatment continues to evolve, with many clinicians following the published, peer-reviewed guidelines recommending a multi-pronged approach: treating underlying infection, reducing inflammation and addressing immune dysfunction, and utilizing psychological and psychiatric therapies as needed. In addition, parents report finding relief with nutrition, supplements, and stress reduction, though these are often employed as additional or complementary, rather than primary, therapies.

As you and your family work through the complexities of your treatment plan, keep the following recommendations in mind:

— *Continue to consult up-to-date resources.* Research into PANDAS and PANS, as well as comorbid conditions and related illnesses, continues to develop, with over a hundred peer-reviewed studies in the past five years alone. Consult reputable sources such as the PANDAS Physicians Network for the most current information about diagnosis and treatment.

— *Seek clarity from your provider about when you may be able to expect improvement.* As PANDAS and PANS are complex disorders, it may take weeks or sometimes months to see significant improvement; some experienced providers may be able to tell you when you can expect symptoms to begin to resolve. If you are not seeing improvements within the expected timeframe, be diligent about follow-up to determine why.

— *Be mindful of effects as you integrate new therapies.* As you transition from one antibiotic to another, for example, or as you begin steroid therapy prescribed by your neurologist, pay close attention to changes in your child's functioning. Report changes in any of your treatment regimens to all providers—even if that means leaving a message at the office or sending a brief heads-up through the patient portal. For example, if your neurologist changes your antibiotic, be sure to notify your nutritionist or gastroenterologist. If your psychiatrist increases the dose of a particular medication, notify your rheumatologist or general pediatrician so that they have up-to-date records as well. This is particularly important in the event of an emergency—should you find yourself in that position, you will not want to be scrambling to remember which provider has what information.

5

Managing Disruptive Behavior and Safety Planning

It was the third week in a row that eight-year-old Kai had threatened his family. This time, he did so while brandishing the one kitchen knife his dad had forgotten to put away in a locked cupboard. Exhausted and afraid for their other children's safety, Kai's parents called 911. By the time the police arrived, Kai had calmed down and was sitting on the floor sobbing. "We're fine now," Kai's mother told the officer. "I just don't know what to do anymore."

The symptoms of PANDAS or PANS (or related versions of autoimmune encephalitis) can overwhelm a family. Not only are the symptoms often severe in nature, but their sudden onset finds parents dealing with behaviors they may not feel they have the skills to manage. This can be terrifying and confusing, and may cause conflict in the home as parents are trying to figure out how best to handle these changes in their child and may not always agree on the best ways to do this. This chapter will address foundational knowledge, skills, and strategies that can assist parents, care providers, and educators in managing these disruptive behaviors in the home and classroom settings. The resources and information presented in this chapter are drawn from multiple sources, including the knowledge and experience of a behavior specialist and crisis management professional on our authorship team who draws on her own background and her training as a crisis response specialist. Many of the strategies shared here have come from training received as a Right Response instructor. Right Response is an organization which offers numerous helpful resources that are widely available and free (Right Response 2018). In this chapter, you will read about:

- the stress cycle and stress response
- triggers to avoid and principles of de-escalation
- use of restraint
- information about recovery and crisis support.

In addition, a simple safety plan template is presented in the Appendix.

Stress cycle

The stress cycle begins with the presentation of a triggering event that causes a stress response. Depending on how an individual manages their stress response, he or she may experience a loss of self-control, resulting in an "alarm state" that may include extreme behaviors. Eventually, the alarm state subsides; the individual regains self-control, goes through an exhaustion stage, and returns to baseline. It is important that an individual return to baseline after a stress response before they try to re-engage or the stress response may be re-triggered, causing another alarm state (see Figure 5.1 for a visual depiction of this process).

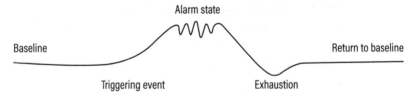

Figure 5.1: Alarm state and return to baseline

Stress response

Stress, simply put, is a biological and psychological response to the perception that an individual does not have the "skills or strategies to deal with the demands of the environment" (McLeod 2010). This demand could be a request to do something, being told "no," seeing a bug, worrisome thoughts, or any number of things. This triggering event is perceived by the body as a threat which initiates a fight or flight response. In our children with PANDAS/PANS/AE, this response is likely something we've not seen before when presented with these triggering events. In other words, things that didn't use to cause a stress response now do. Furthermore, our child's behavior during their stress response may trigger a stress response in us, which further exacerbates the situation.

Let's look at what is happening in the body (Harvard Health 2018; Samartano 2018). With a perceived threat, our senses send a message to the amygdala, the part of the brain responsible for processing emotions. When the amygdala is triggered, it sends a signal to the hypothalamus and pituitary gland, two sections of the brain "responsible for maintaining…balance" throughout your system (Samartano 2018). The hypothalamus communicates with the rest of the body through the autonomic nervous system, which has two components, the sympathetic nervous system and the parasympathetic nervous system. The sympathetic nervous system acts like the "gas pedal" in a car. It triggers the fight or flight response, giving the body a burst of energy so that it can respond to the perceived threat. The adrenal glands pump the hormone epinephrine, also known as adrenaline, into the bloodstream. As epinephrine circulates throughout the body it brings on a number of physiological changes, which may include increased heart rate, blood pressure, breathing, and energy. While choreographed by our body systems, this response occurs so rapidly we may not be aware of it or, worse, may feel it is happening beyond our control. When managed well, this response is a good thing. It allows our heightened senses to help us act quickly to get out of danger and away from the perceived threat. When managed poorly, this response leaves us feeling emotionally flooded and overwhelmed, resulting in any number of undesirable behaviors.

When children with PANDAS and PANS are unable to manage or interrupt this response, due in part to the inflammation in the basal ganglia, it may continue for an extended period of time. It falls on parents and care providers to support them effectively and, equally important, to manage our own stress response. We cannot control the stress response of others, but we can influence it by projecting calm assurance. We do this in several ways.

Understanding our own response to stress

The first step in managing our stress response is to identify that we are having one. We may feel tightness in our chest, nausea, an increase in heart rate, sweaty palms, a lump in our throat, muscular twitching, or any other feelings of an adrenaline rush. At this time, when you notice these symptoms, stop and take a moment to assess your state of mind. What we think about a situation affects our emotional and physiological responses. We can use positive self-talk to help us reduce our stress response. Telling ourselves that we have the skills and strategies to handle the situation will activate the parasympathetic nervous system, which acts like the brakes in a car, dampening the arousal state. Pairing breathing techniques with positive self-talk is also effective in regaining control over our stress response.

In order to influence the stress response of our child, we want to assess our paralanguage, the nonverbal ways we communicate (University of Minnesota Libraries Publishing 2018). Paralanguage includes the physical, nonverbal means of communication that may accompany our spoken words: gestures, facial reactions and expressions, vocal volume, pitch and tone, eye contact, and body position. Our paralanguage should communicate calm support to our child. A relaxed body, neutral face, low and slow voice, slow movements, and downcast eyes can all help to communicate support and assurance. Our paralanguage, as much as (or perhaps even more than) our spoken words, should be nonconfrontational in order to positively influence and reduce the stress response in our child.

Next, we want to try to see the situation through the perception of our child. What is it that they are experiencing? We may not be able to determine this in the moment, but once the child is returned to baseline, we can talk calmly to them to help us get a better understanding of what they are experiencing—this may help in the next instance of similar behavior. We can ask clarifying questions and summarize what we hear them telling us. During this process, we don't interrupt or correct their experience based on our own observations. Rather, we validate their experience as real to them in that moment. Using phrases like "I hear you saying," or "Let me make sure I've got this right," communicates validation and support. Even if what they experienced is different from what we observed, we are communicating support so that we can better understand their perception of the situation. Being empathetic to their experience helps us to be in control of our own stress response as we support them through theirs.

Responding to stress response to prevent challenging behaviors

A behavioral crisis occurs when the behavioral problem exceeds the resources available. These resources may include time, attention, knowledge, and skills. By increasing our resources, we decrease the frequency of crisis. This is not to say that our child's behavioral response decreases, but we are no longer feeling that we are in crisis because we have the knowledge, skills, time, and attention to manage the situation.

There are several things we can do to increase our resources. We can seek out supports, increase our knowledge and skills, and implement systems. Family, friends, and trusted neighbors can all provide support through helping with errands, child care, house cleaning, and other identified tasks. Allowing these things to be taken care of by others decreases the draw on our energy reserves, helping us to better manage ourselves during a stressful situation. Community supports that we may consider accessing include mental health professionals, medical providers, school personnel, and police. When accessing community supports, it is helpful to have a response plan and family safety plan. Mental health professionals can provide individual and family counseling. Finding a professional who is knowledgeable about PANDAS, PANS, or autoimmune encephalitis is ideal but not always possible. If you are not able to find someone knowledgeable about these conditions, seek out a professional who specializes in supporting families dealing with a chronic illness.

Putting together a team of medical professionals may be challenging if you live in an area that doesn't have knowledgeable providers. Seek out local parent support groups to guide you in this process and check the PANDAS Physician Network and PANDAS Network sites for provider lists. Utilize resources to educate schools found at the PANDAS Network site and share with school personnel your response plan. If your child's behaviors become so extreme that you may need to call the police to assist, contact them ahead of time and share your safety plan so they can be prepared and are able to offer maximum support when responding to any future episodes.

Triggers to avoid

As mentioned, managing our own stress response is a skill that will help us more successfully manage a behavioral response in our child.

But there are other things we can do as well. First, there are common triggers we should avoid. For example, it is best to avoid the phrases "Calm down" or "You need to…" These phrases only elicit an increased response from our children and are not likely to be constructive. Think of a time when you were distressed and someone told you to calm down or that you needed to do something else. How did it make you feel? These two phrases do not communicate support or empathy to the individual who is stressed, and therefore they will likely increase the alarm state.

We also want to avoid telling our child what they should *not* do. At this time, they cannot problem solve to determine what they should do, and therefore telling them what not to do leaves them without a solution. Instead, tell them what they can do that is safe and calming. Examples of this might be "Take a breath with me," "Rest your hands," or "Walk with me." These are all statements that tell the child something they can do that is safe and may help them regain self-control.

Avoid blaming, shaming, or rehashing the incident with your child. This only incites the stress response. They are not doing these things on purpose; they are in an out-of-control state. Blaming, shaming, reminding them how disappointed we are, or reminding them how hard we worked to help them will not help to reduce a stress response. We also want to avoid minimizing or contradicting their experience. This does not communicate support or validation. It is important to remember that their experience is real to them in that moment, even if their concerns seem irrational to us. Last, avoid arguing or engaging in a power struggle. Remember that they are not in control of their reasoning at this time. If you are feeling that you need to "win," then you are engaged and should instead take a break yourself.

The behavior exhibited by a stressed child may appear to be intentional and in control; parents often say, in frustration, that they feel their children are manipulating them in tantrums or crisis situations. It is essential to remember that they are having a stress response and cannot control the behaviors they are exhibiting in that moment. Avoid threatening a consequence for that behavior. We are only setting them up for failure when we do that. Our child would problem solve a better response if they could. They can't in that moment, and we will likely not want to implement the threatened consequence afterwards, but may feel that we need to. It is better not to threaten a consequence in the first place.

Finally, avoid restarting the confrontation by immediately demanding emotionally challenging tasks once your child has calmed down. Asking a child to apologize or talk about how they are feeling immediately after an incident is likely out of their capacity. When we are certain that they have returned to baseline, we may want to interview them (in other words, initiate an objective, nonjudgmental conversation about the experience) in order to better understand their experience, but not to elicit an apology. For a child returning to baseline after a crisis state, our role is to support them emotionally and to help them feel that we love them and are there for them. There is certainly a time and place to reinforce appropriate behavioral expectations and address inappropriate actions—but it is not in the immediate aftermath of a crisis episode.

Principles of de-escalation

In addition to avoiding specific triggers, there are strategies we can use to help de-escalate an individual. Always use short, simple directions. When the body is experiencing a stress response its ability to reason is reduced. Providing simple directions helps to minimize the reasoning task on the brain. Give the child time to regain self-control, removing time constrains whenever possible. You may not have control over such things as a doctor's appointment, but you don't have to mention the time constraint during an exacerbation. Simply support the child without putting on any time demands. Providing space can also help to de-escalate a child. Giving them breathing room can minimize the pressure or demands and allow them to regain self-control.

Redirecting a child's attention onto something different can be a useful de-escalation strategy. This can be anything different, or it can be something that is highly desirable. Sometimes, offering choices can be helpful, as long as making a choice is not stressful (it may be challenging for some children with OCD symptoms). Choices can give an individual power and control over a situation. It is important, if you provide choices, that the choices offered are desirable and easy for your child and that you are okay with any of the options your child may select. Also, whenever possible, give a child a way out to avoid embarrassment if they are in a public setting or with peers. Losing control is never fun and never feels good; saving face is important, particularly for children who are around peers or another audience whose opinion means a great deal. Allowing access to a quiet place to de-escalate is a great way to allow a child to save face, whether it's a bedroom in the home, or a quiet space in a school. Make sure that space is safe and free from anything that might be used for self-harm.

Always problem solve with the child. They cannot access the logical executive part of their brain due to their alarm state; therefore, you must be their surrogate brain. Come up with one or more solutions and offer those with your support. For example, if a child is escalated because you've asked them to turn off their electronic device, problem solve with them by suggesting they ask for a little more time to finish. Teach them to "give a little to get a little" and show that "we all give a little" by allowing them more time when they appropriately ask for it.

Sometimes being silent and just being present with an escalated child can be enough to help them de-escalate. Our children with PANDAS or PANS, or other forms of autoimmune encephalitis, can become so distraught that we are not able to console them or problem solve with them and we just sit with them, keeping them safe, assuring them that we love them, and that we are there to help them. Maintaining calm and neutral paralanguage helps to communicate this message of support.

Use of restraint

Restraining an individual who is having a stress response will always increase that response. As their fight or flight response is activated, they are likely to struggle more and may become combative. Restraint should never be used to punish a child, to teach a lesson, or to prevent a non-harmful behavior. It is not a best practice, or even an acceptable practice, to restrain because of non-compliance. Restraint should only be used to protect the aggressive child or others. Institutional guidelines should be followed, if restraint occurs within an institutional setting, and restraint should only be done by individuals who are well trained in the technique. Whenever restraint is used, constantly monitor the child, assessing their vital signs, and avoid constriction of breathing and circulation. If you find that you need to restrain your child for safety reasons, consider asking your school district or mental health professionals if they provide training. Restraint should be used as little as possible. Whenever a child can be allowed a quiet space to de-escalate, that is preferred over restraint, even if there are messes to clean up afterwards. Above all, keep in mind that the best way to prevent the use of restraint is to utilize all of our other skills and strategies.

Box 5.1: Triggers to avoid

- Avoid the terms "Calm down" and "You need to..."

- Avoid the words "no," "not," or any contraction of "not" (e.g. don't, shouldn't).

- Avoid threatening the consequence of a misbehavior.

- Avoid blaming/shaming or rehashing the incident in front of your child.

- Avoid minimizing or contradicting.

- Avoid arguing or engaging in a power struggle.

- Avoid restarting the confrontation by immediately demanding emotionally difficult actions.

Box 5.2: Principles of de-escalation

- Use short, simple words, phrases, and directions.

- *Time*: Give the person time to cope and remove time demands whenever possible.

- *Space*: Give the person breathing room to minimize the pressure or demands.

- *Redirect*: Shift the person's thoughts or actions to something different or a more productive and alternative way to cope.

- *Choices*: Give or suggest options that allow the person to have control over the situation.

- *Open a door*: Give the person a way out, to save face or minimize embarrassment.

- *Problem solve*: Help the person identify solutions to manage themselves.

- *Silence*: Use silence to help de-escalate the situation.

Recovery

As your child heals, the exacerbations will likely decrease in severity and intensity. During this process, you will re-introduce expectations and events that have most likely been removed to avoid the stress response. At the same time, you can begin to reinforce more functional and successful behaviors, replacing the disruptive and challenging ones. Additionally, your child will likely be more amenable to accessing cognitive behavioral therapy with a provider they trust and can work with. This will begin the process of teaching them alternative thought processes to interrupt the stress response. Take advantage of other resources for continued healing as well. The WRAP, or Wellness Recovery Action Plan (Copeland 2018), is an excellent tool for anyone, at any time, and for any of life's challenges. The entire family can benefit from utilizing these resources for recovery. Most importantly, begin to celebrate life again.

Conclusion and key points

Managing our own stress response is vital to influencing the stress response of others, including our children. While it feels overwhelming to have a child in crisis, and severe exacerbations can easily lead to crisis episodes, there is hope, and recovery does lie ahead. Seeking out appropriate support, in our experience and as reported anecdotally from many parents, can be essential to getting through this challenging time. You do not need to do this alone.

As you support your child through periods of crisis, the following reminders may be particularly useful:

— Avoiding triggers and utilizing de-escalation strategies will help a child regain self-control.

— Increasing our resources through self-care, utilizing supports in our life, and increasing our knowledge and skills will help us feel confident and capable.

— Seeking out community resources will help us gain these skills and connect us with others who may be experiencing similar situations.

6

Challenges in Finding and Accessing Treatment

When Alexander first began exhibiting anxiety, counting compulsively and lining objects up, his mother, a third-grade teacher, assumed he had autism. His pediatrician agreed, referred them to a psychologist, and made some notes in six-year-old Alexander's chart. It was not until two years later, when his behaviors escalated and he became violent, that a different psychologist, taking a complete medical history prior to inpatient intake, made the connection between recurrent strep infections at age six and the onset of obsessive-compulsive symptoms six weeks later. The relief Alexander's mother felt at having a diagnosis was quickly tempered by her realization that this psychologist, while sympathetic, was unable to prescribe medication to treat PANDAS. Alexander's pediatrician remained unfamiliar with PANDAS and seemed uninterested in learning more, shrugging it off as "controversial" and "rare." The one specialist who seemed able to help, suggested by the sympathetic psychologist, practiced two states away and did not take insurance. Reluctantly, his mother, a single parent, took out a credit card that was already close to its limit and crossed her fingers that she had enough remaining on it to book the appointment.

"Seeing is believing" is a common phrase used by parents of children afflicted with PANDAS/PANS, as well as (in our anecdotal experience) some providers. However, despite the clear presentation of symptoms, parents can have extreme difficulty finding a qualified treatment provider. This is the case because the diagnosis of PANDAS or PANS is a clinical diagnosis (Chang *et al.* 2015; NIMH n.d.) and one of exclusion, open to interpretation and subjective observation. For this reason, identification depends on a careful and thorough medical history, consideration of psychosocial development, physical exam and supportive labs, and most importantly, a physician or therapist knowledgeable about PANDAS. This process can be time-consuming, expensive and uncertain. In this chapter, we review some of the common challenges in finding diagnosis and treatment, and we offer suggestions to parents as they navigate this process.

Barriers to diagnosis and treatment

Unfortunately, many doctors still believe PANDAS or PANS do not exist or are too controversial to treat. Some pediatricians who are open to the idea of PANDAS/PANS simply do not know how to treat, and refer the case to a known specialist, possibly creating wait times of several months for an appointment. Specialists treating this disorder are scarce, and families frequently resort to traveling back and forth to other states for help.

In addition, the structure of our healthcare system can create barriers for children and families affected by this complex, multifaceted disorder. Our current medical system frequently divides patients into groups, one being mental health and the other being medical health. However, PANDAS and PANS are medical in terms of cause but neurological and psychiatric in terms of symptoms. Often, medical doctors and mental health clinicians fail to communicate or collaborate with one another, so these children are often misdiagnosed, most likely receiving a diagnosis that very much depends on the training or medical orientation of the treating physician. Families, who may be in crisis, often arrive in an emergency room, pediatrician's or psychiatrist's office, where the staff have little, if any, knowledge of PANDAS or PANS. At that point, particularly for a child in an acute or dangerous exacerbation, parents may be under too much stress to effectively articulate reasons to consider a PANDAS/PANS diagnosis, and clinicians may be so focused on stabilizing the child's symptoms that they are unprepared for a fuller discussion of underlying causes.

Given the overlap of symptoms with many other psychiatric disorders, children with PANDAS/PANS may be at a high risk of receiving an inaccurate mental health diagnosis and receiving

Challenges in Finding and Accessing Treatment   63

ineffective treatment interventions as a result. Symptoms overlap with those of several well-known psychiatric disorders, such as OCD, anxiety, Tourette's syndrome, ADHD, depression, oppositional defiant disorder, bipolar disorder, autism, and post-traumatic stress disorder (PTSD), making it challenging for doctors to diagnose accurately.

The acute onset of symptoms is the hallmark sign of PANDAS (Chang 2015; Kovacevic n.d.), but some children are often frightened by their own behavior and may work hard to hide these bizarre changes. In such cases, the initial onset may be missed, possibly delaying treatment as well as obscuring diagnosis. In some cases, there may be an occult or hidden strep infection (and therefore unnoticed and untreated) as strep can be hiding and thriving in other parts of the body besides the throat, such as sinuses, stomach, genitals, and anus (NIMH n.d.).

Furthermore, PANDAS/PANS symptoms most often do not present until several weeks to months after the initial infection, making the clinical connection between the two even harder to identify. As with many autoimmune disorders, there is no conclusive test for PANDAS/PANS (NIMH n.d.); laboratory results can help but can be hard to track accurately and can be inconclusive. Cultures or blood titer levels to check for streptococcal or other infection can be ordered (Chang *et al.* 2015), but results frequently vary and, if inconclusive, still can lead to a missed diagnosis. More advanced and accurate testing, such as the Cunningham Panel offered by Moleculera Labs (Moleculera 2018), a series of five immune marker tests, is an option, but it takes two to three weeks for results and the cost is, thus far, not consistently covered by insurance.

Given all of these factors, it is not always easy for a doctor to determine a diagnosis of PANDAS. PANDAS symptoms relapse and remit (come and go) (NIMH n.d.), which can cause further difficulty in diagnosis. It may even seem to doctors that parents are exaggerating or fabricating symptoms based on this confusing pattern. Symptoms may also mistakenly give the appearance of having a psychosocial, trauma, or parenting trigger, leading again to a missed underlying medical cause. Unfortunately, some parents have been accused of inappropriate decision-making on their children's behalf, or even medical neglect (Sorel 2016). As a parent, try not to take it personally if suggestions of poor parenting or misperception on your part are raised by clinicians, who are in all likelihood simply seeking the best outcome for your child even if they have a different perspective. However, bear in mind that you do have the right to seek other treatment providers if you do not feel you are receiving a compassionate, collaborative, or effective response from clinicians.

Another challenge in accessing treatments is that the recommended treatments for the disorder are not consistently covered by medical insurance. Often, families engage in a high-stress battle with insurance companies, due to the lack of coverage, for the most effective yet very expensive treatment methods. Too many families have lost their homes and savings to fund necessary lifesaving but costly healing (Sorel 2016). Fortunately, the passing of a law in Illinois in 2017, mandating medical insurance providers to cover necessary specific treatment of PANDAS/PANS, has helped to ensure increased access to treatment; other states in the United States (such as Delaware) have worked to pass similar laws or are engaging in similar advocacy efforts at this time.

While this disorder has been recognized by experts for decades, the link between the symptoms and a common childhood illness has also been the subject of intense controversy, with some doctors claiming insufficient evidence and denying suffering children critical early treatment to fight the sometimes elusive infection. For over 20 years following the discovery, PANDAS/PANS have had no medical code acknowledged by the International Classification of Diseases (ICD) manual, contributing to the lack of training and awareness of the disorder among physicians and therapists. This fact will soon change, as the 11th edition of the ICD (ICD-11) will finally contain a code for PANDAS.

Currently it is estimated that parents will see an average of eight doctors and spend three years seeking a correct diagnosis due to the present lack of awareness (PANDAS Network 2018). If left untreated during this time, the possible permanent neurological damage and years of developmental disruption to the child cannot be ignored. Informed parents know their children and often are still unable to convince physicians to acknowledge or treat this disorder. With PANDAS and PANS, the parent is often the driving force, desperately seeking to get back their previously normal functioning child. Many families have found support by reaching out to local PANDAS/PANS advocacy groups or, in the U.S., utilizing the PANDAS Network website to find PANDAS-knowledgeable treatment providers listed by state. These children can heal, but early intervention and treatment are crucial. By increasing awareness and acceptance among the medical and mental health community, parents can be empowered to make this often misdiagnosed and misunderstood condition a curable illness, instead of a lifetime of preventable suffering.

Conclusion and key points

PANDAS/PANS is a clinical diagnosis with no conclusive tests and depends on a careful thorough examination of medical history and psychosocial development, physical exam, supportive labs, and most importantly an informed and knowledgeable physician or therapist. PANDAS/PANS is medical in its cause, but neurological and psychiatric in its symptoms. It truly takes a multidisciplinary collaboration among treatment providers to identify and most effectively treat. Due to the range and overlap of symptoms, PANDAS/PANS is often misdiagnosed, and children are at a high risk of receiving an inaccurate mental health diagnosis and inappropriate treatment interventions.

— Parents are encouraged to remain calm while seeking a correct diagnosis. Remaining calm will allow you to collect and present medical symptoms and facts in a convincing manner, facilitating communication with providers.

— Look for knowledgeable and compassionate physicians and be prepared to seek multidisciplinary treatment providers for collaboration of interventions.

— Reach out to local advocacy groups for support and information on knowledgeable treatment providers.

7

Managing Relapse and Recovery

George and Kanisha, parents of two children with PANS, drained their retirement accounts to pay for IVIG for both children after they both became ill at the same time. After a year of homebound school, repeat infusions of IVIG, prophylactic antibiotics, and vigilance about any exposure to infection, both their son and daughter had attained a point of stability where symptoms were low-grade and quite manageable. One night, Kanisha, who was their full-time caregiver during the workday, brought up the question of returning the children to school. "After all," she said, "I'd get a lot more work done, and they can't be isolated from the world forever." George shook his head. "We spent all this time getting them to this point," he said. "We have come so far…and besides, we're out of money. What would we do if one of them got exposed to something at school and we had to do this all over again?"

Preventing relapse

For many parents, particularly those who have arrived at a hard-won place of health and stability, the primary goal may be to prevent any relapse. It is worth noting that PANDAS and PANS are characterized as having a "relapsing/remitting" course (NIMH n.d.); therefore, particularly for children beginning the treatment process, avoiding relapse entirely may not be realistic. Anecdotally, some parents report having children who experience repeat episodes, both before and after beginning treatment, and studies have borne this out as well (Calaprice *et al.* 2017b). As a caregiver, therefore, it may be important to know that relapse in any chronic or long-term illness is not always avoidable and is not your "fault."

That being said, some parents report utilizing strategies to minimize risk of re-exposure or illness. As with other elements of this book, these strategies are shared by parents and should not be considered to constitute medical advice; always follow the guidance of your healthcare team in managing symptoms and avoiding exposure to potential triggers for illness. These strategies, gathered from parent feedback and personal experience, are outlined below for consideration and further discussion with your qualified medical providers.

Manage exposure carefully in the affected child

For children in the immediate post-infectious phase, whether on prophylactic antibiotic medicine or not, this step may involve reducing outside activities; limiting time spent in school or limiting exposure to illness while in school; and carefully screening playmates and peers.

Returning to school is often a goal and a marker of recovery for many children and families. At the same time, school settings can prevent unique challenges in that they group large numbers of students, who may or may not be in various stages of illness, together in close proximity (Candelaria-Greene 2016). Often, during the winter months especially, illnesses can spread rapidly in school settings. Some ideas for limiting exposure to illness for children who are attending school regularly are provided below:

- *Request special assistance with cleaning, according to your district's protocol.* This may involve having an adult sanitize surfaces before your child enters the room; having custodial staff make extra visits to your child's classroom; giving your child consistent access to sanitizing products and antibacterial wipes; and the like.

- *Carefully consider your child's seat.* Sitting in a group of five, facing four other students, may place your child at risk for exposure to every sneeze or cough. Work with your child's teachers and the school nurse to determine the most appropriate seating arrangement that will minimize exposure to germs while also allowing your child to be part of the classroom and interact in socially appropriate ways. You may find that the balance between these two goals changes as your child's health status evolves; a student who is three years out from acute illness may be able to sit with peers as usual, while a child recovering from a significant episode may need more flexible seating arrangements.

- *During high-exposure seasons, consider flexible scheduling.* Some students and families report success with modified schedules, attending school less frequently during flu season, for example. Others, particularly at the high school level, carefully arrange their daily schedule to allow for additional sleep or mealtimes at home in order to support general health.

- *Ensure all adults working with your student are aware of his or her health needs* (Candelaria-Greene 2016). All adults who come into contact with your child should be aware of his or her unique need to avoid exposure to illness. This may impact, for example, who your child sits with at lunch, whether your child is asked to sit in a desk that has not been cleaned, and similar decisions. In addition, adults working with your child in close proximity should be aware of potential risk to your child from any illness they may be carrying. School districts generally cannot require employees to disclose their own health information to parents and must balance your child's healthcare needs with staff privacy and employment rights. For example, you are unlikely to be successful if you ask everyone in the building to be tested for strep carrier status. However, you should impress upon your child's team that your child is not well served by exposure to a staff member who might come to work with a fever. Work proactively and respectfully with the school nurse and school leadership (and district leadership if need be) to identify alternatives that will allow your child to receive needed services when staff members may be ill.

Box 7.1: Maribel's occupational therapy

Maribel, age seven, receives two half-hour occupational therapy sessions weekly for fine motor issues resulting from a severe PANS exacerbation the year prior. Maribel's parents have a strong relationship with her occupational therapist, and because of the severity of her illness last year, they have made it clear that limiting her exposure to bacteria and viruses is a priority for them. One week in February, the therapist calls Maribel's parents to let them know her own young children have been diagnosed with flu. While she is currently symptom-free, they make the decision together to delay Maribel's therapy services for the next two weeks in order to minimize potential exposure to flu, with make-up sessions to be scheduled at a later date. This arrangement, which technically places the therapist out of compliance with Maribel's educational plan in the short term, is possible because the partnership between Maribel's family and her therapist is marked by strong communication on both sides, mutual trust, and flexibility.

Manage exposure carefully with respect to family members and close friends

It may be a sensitive topic, but when your child is in an acute phase of illness or in recovery, exposure to individuals who may be ill can increase their likelihood of infection or illness exacerbation. This may mean family members—cousins, grandparents, aunts, and uncles—and close friends must be circumspect about spending time in proximity to your child. Some families report making difficult decisions regarding attendance at family parties, holiday gatherings, and the like. If you fall into this category, know that you are not alone and that other families have dealt with similar dilemmas. Should you have questions about whether a specific event would involve unhealthy or dangerous exposure for your child, contact your PANDAS specialist for advice if possible.

If indicated by your healthcare team, consider any potential role of allergens or food intolerances

Some individuals with autoimmunity appear to attain improved health with specialized diets such as gluten-free or dairy-free regimens. Should your child fall into this category, you may find that, even beyond the recovery process, it is beneficial to continue a specialized diet or health regimen to avoid potential triggers of illness. Some parents report consulting with gastroenterologists or nutritionists in addition to their primary PANDAS/PANS specialists. (As always, if your child has restricted eating behaviors, be mindful of potential interactions between dietary limitations and disordered eating, and discuss changes in eating behaviors with your healthcare team as needed.)

Ask your healthcare team about steps and strategies to strengthen your child's immune system if appropriate

Recent studies have found deficiencies in some vitamins and minerals among children with PANDAS, such as vitamin D (Celik *et al.* 2016). As you begin transitioning to recovery and a prevention-based mindset, ask your healthcare provider if you should consider any additional steps to strengthen your child's immune system and reduce the risk of exposure to illness.

Managing ongoing disease and transitioning to a new state of health

The peer-reviewed treatment guidelines published in 2017 detail recommendations for treating initial and recurrent episodes of PANDAS or PANS (Cooperstock *et al.* 2017; Frankovich *et al.* 2017; Thienemann *et al.* 2017). You may find, during relapse, the same therapies are effective again that were effective initially. Some families recount moving to progressively more intensive therapies, such as IVIG and plasmapheresis, if the recurrence is severe.

As your child recovers, you will need to thoughtfully communicate with your family members and mental health providers, if your family is using any, to transition to a new state of health. You may find that your routines need to change; for example, your morning routine may have involved carefully managing your second-grader's schedule to get her to school on time, but now you need to build in additional time to administer prophylactic medications and supplements.

Consider questions such as the following in evaluating and planning for any changes in routine:

- Does our wakeup routine or morning routine need to be evaluated?

- Do we need to build in additional time through various points in the day for medication administration?

- Does transportation (to school or childcare) take additional time?

- How often do we need to plan for doctor, nurse practitioner, or therapist visits?

- Do our mealtime routines need to change in any way (additional time for eating, seating arrangements, etc.)?

- Do our bedtime routines need to be re-evaluated?

Most of all, be flexible; any and all of your carefully chosen routines may be subject to change if you notice a recurrence of symptoms. See Box 7.2 for an example of how Foster's family dealt with a recurrence of symptoms.

Box 7.2: Foster's relapse and recovery

Monija, a single mother to Foster, age seven, had battled through his initial episode and diagnosis 18 months ago. After a traumatic year that included an inpatient hospitalization for Foster and several rounds of IVIG, she felt the two of them were finally reaching a point of stability. However, as winter approached, Foster caught the inevitable cold and, three weeks later, began displaying the tics and oppositional behaviors that had characterized his first episode. Monija called her PANDAS specialist and took the earliest possible appointment.

Conclusion and key points

Frequently, parents find that PANDAS and PANS can stress their family in unexpected ways, especially when it comes to managing relapse and adapting to new conceptions of "normal." Children may appear to backslide or may experience full-blown relapse, particularly during winter months when exposure to illness is more frequent. Typically, PANDAS and PANS specialists are prepared for this eventuality and will be able to guide you in formulating a treatment plan for any new manifestations of illness. As you adapt to this new reality, keep the following in mind:

- Don't be afraid to take proactive steps to safeguard your child's health.

- Additionally, be willing to take action quickly if you notice symptoms returning.

- The routines and coping mechanisms you put in place may be subject to frequent revision and re-evaluation, particularly if you notice a return of symptoms.

- Should your child relapse (which is, unfortunately, likely, especially early in recovery), be proactive about consulting your physician early and putting any necessary changes or supports into place.

2

Living Well with PANDAS and PANS Symptoms

8

Emotional and Behavioral Impact

MANAGING MENTAL HEALTH SYMPTOMS ON A DAY-TO-DAY BASIS

Robert, a 17-year-old who was diagnosed with PANS at 14, has just come home from his third inpatient psychiatric hospitalization. His parents and his medical team acknowledge that his behaviors are medically driven, but in times of intense exacerbation, they have found no other option to keep Robert's three siblings physically safe during his lengthy and violent episodes of rage. Having been stabilized during inpatient treatment, Robert is looking forward to being home and continuing his recovery. However, his parents still struggle with finding and implementing appropriate strategies. "I'm glad to be out of the crisis phase again," his mom writes in her journal, "but I'm not sure how to continue managing hour by hour and day by day."

For families such as Robert's, it can be difficult to transition from the acute crisis phase to formulating and implementing a structured routine that will support their child's social and behavioral functioning. In particular, parents sometimes report challenges making the shift from "crisis mode" to "ongoing maintenance and targeting behaviors." This chapter presents some suggestions and strategies, vetted by mental health clinicians and social work experts, for supporting social and emotional functioning, day in and day out, in children in recovery from PANDAS and PANS.

As a parent, you must first take into consideration whether your child is in an acute phase of illness or a healing phase of illness.

Understanding the difference will significantly change how you can better navigate these symptoms.

During acute illness

During the acute phase of illness, your child's behaviors are a direct result of their medical condition. This may be a child who has been misdiagnosed for several years or a child who is in a temporary flare due to a new strep (or other) infection. Since the symptomology is medically induced you cannot expect traditional behavioral methods to be successful.

During an acute phase of illness, it is best to try to establish good boundaries and safe conditions, and identify new (and hopefully temporary) definitions of normal. By doing this, you can reduce additional stress which can be caused by setting up unrealistic expectations.

Setting effective boundaries

Take advantage of any down time to communicate with your child. Processes and procedures for communicating, as well as ideal times of day, will significantly vary from one child to the next, so you will need to discover when this may work for you. It is during these calmer times that you can take advantage of healthy and direct communication. Talk with your child about the fact that their behaviors are not their fault, but that some behaviors are still unacceptable, and you would like to formulate a plan to address them going forward. Examples may include:

- physical aggression
- inappropriate language
- threatening self or others
- attempting to use household items as weapons
- leaving the home unannounced and/or unsupervised.

It would be best to try to process these concerns as often as they come up, using nonconfrontational and calm language as described in our earlier discussion of crisis management. This way, when your child enters into the healing phase, they will already know which coping skills to maintain and which to change.

Creating safe conditions

One difficult symptom of living with PANDAS/PANS is physical aggression. Creating a safe environment is important for the entire family as siblings are often the target of verbal and/or physical aggression.

For younger children

If you have an extra room in the home, create a safe place. Such a room would have minimal toys, books, or other items which can be destroyed or used as weapons. You may want to include a radio if your child finds music calming, or television if this has been a source of comfort. Be sure to not have too many visual stimuli (as many of these children also suffer from sensory issues). Also include lots of soft, comforting items such as blankets, pillows, stress toys, stuffed animals and/or weighted blankets. When in a rage, it would be best to take your child to this room to wait out the episode and return to a calmer state.

Sometimes a child's bedroom may be the only possible place for refuge. If this is the case, consider limiting the number of toys and books the child keeps in their room. Keep clutter to a minimum and make sure any toys/items which may become unsafe are removed.

For older children

Creating safe spaces for older children can be much more challenging, as can trying to navigate them to such a space. When your child is in a calm state, have them help you to create their own safe space. Communicate with them during these down times about the importance of the space and the need to try to use it during flares. Again, consider limiting what is in the space to things which you are aware may calm them down.

While creating a safe space for older children is well intentioned, the reality is that many of our acutely ill, older children are larger and/ or stronger than their guardians and, in the throes of a crisis, may not remain in an assigned "safe space." If this is the case, you may consider a safety plan. Identifying friends or relatives who live close by could be helpful when a rage becomes physically unmanageable. And, in any situation where you feel that anyone is at risk of harm, you may need to consider calling emergency services. Make sure you have created a safety plan and, if possible, spoken with first responders in advance so that they are prepared for behaviors and symptoms they may encounter.

For siblings

Even if your child's sibling is not a target of verbal and/or physical aggression they are still witnessing a traumatic event. If having a safe room is not an option in your home, create an exit plan for the sibling. This plan could just include one parent/guardian taking them out of the home, or a relative coming to pick them up. Weather permitting, leaving to take a walk, bike ride, etc. can be helpful. The less a sibling is exposed, the less risk they are at of experiencing PTSD later on and/or taking on negative, learned behaviors they observe in their siblings.

Defining "normal" during illness

When your child is acutely ill, it will be important for you to not hold them to the same expectations you may have had before onset of their illness. For example:

- The child who happily attended dance class once a week without any issue may now refuse to enter the dance room and may sob while grasping at your leg. This is your new normal.

- The child who used to get themselves ready for school without assistance now needs you to watch over their shoulder as they complete each task. This is your new normal.

- The child who used to go to bed in five minutes without hesitation now needs to complete an extensive one-hour bedtime ritual before even considering going to bed. This is your new normal.

- The child who once ate any food you prepared for them may now only eat between three and five foods. This is your new normal. However, if your child develops food restriction, you should seek the help of medical and/or mental health professionals.

The hope, of course, is that these new states of normal are temporary. For many children, some symptomology will dissipate simply with the help of proper medical attention. But until then, it will be pertinent to define, accept, and adjust to the new normal. Behavioral therapies will likely be unsuccessful during this stage of illness and attempting to implement them will only cause more frustration and upset for everyone.

Suggestions for tracking symptoms and case management

As PANDAS and PANS can be unpredictable in their onset, course, and resolution, one way to better navigate symptoms is through developing good case management skills. According to the Case Management Society of America, the formal definition of case management is "a collaborative process of assessment, planning, facilitation, care coordination, evaluation, and advocacy for options and services to meet an individual's and family's comprehensive health needs through communication and available resources to promote quality, cost-effective outcomes" (Case Management Society of America n.d.)

You will come to learn that one of your roles as a caregiver of a child with PANDAS or PANS will also be that of case manager. This can be done using a notebook or weekly planner; there are also apps recently developed for tracking PANS symptoms, as mentioned in Chapter 1, such as *PANDAS/PANS Journal*, which is currently available for iOS. While learning to case manage your child's illness can feel overwhelming and tedious, it will help you to see the big picture of what happens during acute illness versus the healing phase. Each day it could be helpful to track symptomology. Examples of what to track may include but are not limited to:

- tracking severity of symptoms

- tracking length of symptoms

- tracking foods your child will or will not eat

- listing medications they may have taken that day

- tracking onset of any illness, increase in allergy symptoms (if applicable), and/or any illness that you may be aware of going around your child's school

- tracking doctors' appointments and keeping a list of which medications were prescribed by which doctor and when.

Caring for PANDAS, PANS, or any form of AE can often require involving many medical professionals. And as you move from one doctor to the next your medical records may not be accessible. Sorting documents in a separate folder or filing system will help you to navigate new doctors' appointments more efficiently. If your child's medical history is available via online medical charts, print out any relevant documents and create your own paper file. (See Chapter 6 for more discussion of coordinating care among medical professionals; the information provided below is intended as a reminder and recap.)

Important documents to file and maintain, both electronically and in hard copy, may include but are not limited to:

- history of strep and/or other medical concerns

- history of autoimmune disorder

- current medications

- history of medications

- records of immunizations

- any blood test results

- allergy testing and results

- if known and/or available, family history of autoimmune and or mental health concerns

- history of mental health records

- psychiatric evaluation

- mental health assessment

- therapy history, contact information of therapists, and dates of service

- history of mental health medication.

Many children suffering from AE will need the assistance of a 504 plan or Individualized Education Program (IEP) while managing their illness at school (see Chapter 16). If your child receives a 504 plan,[1] IEP or other health-related plan, maintain these documents as well. School-related documents to collect and track may include:

- report cards

- work samples

- handwriting samples

- assessment results (including formal assessments, especially demonstrating changes over time aligned with symptom progression or diagnosis timeline)

- IEP or 504 plans.

During the healing phase

Setting effective boundaries

During the healing phase of the illness, you will likely struggle to find the difference between medical symptomology and residual poor coping skills. We often see that children who are healing from PANDAS/PANS may still have a "short fuse" but their ability to control negative behaviors is improved. Reminding your child of the boundaries set during the acute phase of illness is your first step. Revisit with them all behaviors that are considered unacceptable.

When discussing traditional cognitive behavioral interventions, reward systems are considered more effective than implementing consequences. This is strongly encouraged for children with PANDAS/PANS but may not be the only effective line of intervention. While in the healing phase you may discuss with your child the list of negative symptoms they had experienced and may still continue to struggle with. Discuss with your child what types of rewards would be enticing for them (within reason, of course) and then, together, implement a reward system. Below are two examples.

---

1   "504 plan" is a term used in the United States to refer to a legal document that specifies accommodations or supports provided to an individual with a disability. The protections a 504 plan provides are less extensive than those associated with an Individualized Education Program but still confer civil rights protection, and the legal guarantee of accommodations in some settings, on the individual with a disability.

For a younger child

If a residual symptom includes throwing items when he/she gets angry, work with them on allowing for 30 minutes of screen time (time allowed for cell phones, television, computers, or any other electronic device) for every episode in which they don't throw things when they get angry. Make sure to remind them during an anger episode that being angry is okay, but throwing things is not. Calming down without throwing items will still earn them their screen time.

For an older child

If a residual symptom is fighting about getting ready for school, provide an age-appropriate incentive. You might, for example, arrange for them to earn $5 toward a gift card of their choice for each day they get ready for school without issue. By the end of the week they would have earned a $25 gift card of their choice. Keep in mind, if they struggle for part of the week you would not take away any days earned. So, if they cooperate for three days but struggle for two, they would still have earned a $15 gift card at the end of the week. This allows your children to continue to see incremental progress and—particularly important with the episodic course of PANDAS and PANS—does not place them in an "all or nothing" position when flares, even short-lived ones, occur.

Successful implementation of a reward system requires good communication and follow-through. Try to make all goals realistic and obtainable in a relatively short period of time. If children do not feel the benefits of the reward soon enough, they quickly lose interest in trying to earn them.

Unfortunately, due to the severity and unpredictability of the illness, there are times when you will need to implement consequences as well. Best practice for successful use of consequences includes discussing them ahead of time, making sure the consequence is appropriate for the behavior, and consistent follow-through. Implementing consequences can be difficult due to the nature of this illness but allowing children to continue with unhealthy coping skills can have a long-term effect. If your child is working with a mental health professional, that individual can often be an excellent source of guidance in terms of when it is appropriate to impose consequences and how to do so.

Ultimately, the success of rewards and punishment systems is, in part, due to how we prepare for them (Walters Wright n.d.). Experts suggest several specific strategies for parents, including understanding the nature of rewards and differentiating between tangible and intangible rewards (Walters Wright n.d.), and giving your child a voice in the process so that he or she is empowered to select preferred rewards or weigh in on how and when they should be assigned. Being clear and specific about expectations, terms of reward agreements, and consequences is also important (Walters Wright n.d.). Last, parents should use consequences carefully; try to provide positive rewards far more often than negative consequences but be sure to follow through so that your child sees the reward system implemented with consistency (Walters Wright n.d.).

Last, communicating with school personnel and aligning reward systems across home and school may be valuable in providing additional consistency for your child (Walters Wright n.d.). All of this, however, is subject to the caveat that your child may need a reward system or agreement adjusted during times of crisis and acute exacerbation. Adjusting your approach during such times is not "being weak" or "being inconsistent." Rather, it is recognizing that your child's medical needs may, at times, outrank his or her need for behavioral guidelines. (If your child were in the hospital having open-heart surgery, it's likely you'd feel far less guilt over shelving his or her behavioral plan or rewards chart temporarily!) If you have a PANDAS or PANS-literate medical provider or therapist on your healthcare team, that individual can likely be a good source of information as to when you have crossed the line into that "crisis" mode.

Conclusion and key points

Supporting your child's mental well-being and emotional and behavioral symptoms on a day-to-day basis can be taxing for any parent—particularly for those who may also be dealing with significant medical and financial complexities related to PANDAS or PANS. Being attentive to your child's medical status, working to address symptoms in consistent ways, and remaining flexible during exacerbations are key to re-establishing consistent behavioral expectations. Input from a knowledgeable and experienced health or mental healthcare provider is of critical importance.

As parents, keeping the following strategies in mind may be useful:

— *Document your child's emotional or behavioral symptoms continuously.* As mentioned earlier in this chapter, the use of an app or online tracking system may be particularly helpful.

— *Be willing to ask for assistance when needed.* This may include assistance from your healthcare (including mental healthcare) team, but it may also include assistance from friends and family. There is sometimes a lack of awareness (or even stigma) attached to mental health needs that makes families reluctant to reach out or may prevent friends and family from offering help. Asking for assistance ("John just got home from the hospital; is anyone able to set up a meal train for us this week?" or, "It's been a really hectic week. Could I ask you to pick Maisy up from school this week for me?") can be difficult but worthwhile.

9

Managing OCD on a Daily Basis

Charlie's compulsions became apparent to his mother in piecemeal ways. First, he began clearing his plate at dinner when it was still full, even on nights when she had served his favorite foods, such as spaghetti and pizza. At the same time, she noticed he had accumulated much less dirty laundry in his room, perhaps because he wore the same four or five t-shirts constantly. In fact, he had moved all the other t-shirts in his dresser to the very back of his closet, even though they all still fit. She didn't put the pieces together until the day that Charlie had a 45-minute tantrum over a routine homework assignment that asked him to circle vocabulary words with a red pen. Finally, he verbalized what was bothering him about the homework and about his food and clothing as well: he had an overwhelming need to avoid anything red because he was convinced he would kill his family members if he touched anything that was red.

Obsessive-compulsive disorder (OCD) is a mental health disorder:

> that occurs when a person gets caught in a cycle of obsessions and compulsions. Obsessions are unwanted, intrusive thoughts, images or urges that trigger intensely distressing feelings. Compulsions are behaviors an individual engages in to attempt to get rid of the obsessions and/or decrease his or her distress. (International OCD Foundation n.d.)

In PANDAS, PANS, or autoimmune encephalitis, we often see what is considered a sudden onset of OCD. This means that before the onset of illness the child had no signs or symptoms of OCD; at onset, symptoms of OCD appear, often in a sudden and devastating manner.

Even with sudden onset, you may often see signs of symptomology in hindsight, as Charlie's mother does, particularly if children take pains to hide their symptoms because of their own fear, embarrassment, or confusion. The good news is that many children with PANDAS, PANS, or encephalitis witness a significant decrease in OCD symptoms after receiving proper medical care. Residual symptoms can then be treated accordingly.

OCD can be best managed in the healing phase of your child's illness. The best way to navigate OCD thoughts, behaviors, and rituals is through cognitive behavioral therapy (CBT). CBT "is a short-term, goal-oriented psychotherapy treatment that takes a hands-on, practical approach to problem-solving [in order to] change patterns of thinking or behavior" (Martin 2018). CBT is considered a standard of care for OCD, either alone or in conjunction with other therapies and medications (American Psychiatric Association (APA) 2007).

If your child is beginning CBT, you may find it helpful to attend therapy with him or her, as this will allow you to dialogue with the therapist so that you know how to effectively navigate OCD symptoms at home in accord with your child's treatment plan. Your therapist may also include exposure response prevention (ERP) as part of your child's treatment plan (APA 2007).

Exposure response prevention (ERP)

Effective treatment methods include both exposing a child to an upsetting stimulus ("exposure") and preventing the avoidance behaviors that often follow exposure, forcing the child into the position of engaging with stimuli that may cause anxiety while minimizing avoidance behaviors (Huppert and Roth 2003).

Summarized into parent-friendly language, this simply means that we, as parents, must learn how to help our children face their fears without allowing them to follow through with ritualistic behaviors. In turn, the goal is to teach them that their fears cannot harm them and are, therefore, unrealistic. In full disclosure, accomplishing this as a caregiver is difficult, exhausting, and heartbreaking. But, if you can accomplish this appropriately, it is also necessary and effective. It is strongly recommended you work with your therapist and/or your child's therapist in order to discuss and plan how to implement ERP at home. The extended example on the following pages will help to illustrate this concept.

Implementing ERP at home

A six-year-old diagnosed as having PANDAS was in the healing phase of her illness. Her residual OCD symptoms included excessive hand washing and feeling the need to use the bathroom three times before bed. Working with her mental health team, her parents planned to manage her symptoms at home through a structured ERP program. The program covered the following areas, each of which was discussed with the child as appropriate for her age and developmental status.

Hand washing

The child had to be closely monitored at home to watch for unnecessary hand washing. When the child attempted to wash her hands (for no reason) a parent would intervene, move her away from the bathroom and sit with the child, holding her hands until the need to wash passed. During the ERP the parent would talk with the child about how she would still be okay, even if she did not wash her hands. When the child was able to calm down and report that she would not wash her hands, the parent would let go. However, at times, the child would run back to the sink and the ERP would start over.

Bedtime bathroom use

The child was permitted to use the bathroom one time before bed and informed that she would not be permitted to use the bathroom after her first use. (This protocol was cleared with the child's physician as well to rule out any physical or medical issues, as urinary frequency can be a sign of PANDAS onset or relapse.) In early phases of ERP, the parent would then put the child to bed, remind her of the expectations and then sit in front of the bathroom door. When the child arrived at the bathroom to attempt using the bathroom, the parent would not let her in and would discuss how she will be okay even if she does not use the bathroom. When the child was able to calm down she would be put back to bed. This would be repeated as needed in early ERP. As treatment progressed and the child became more comfortable with waiting to use the bathroom or using it only once, the parent would require the child to stay in the bedroom rather than going to the bathroom.

Challenges in managing OCD day to day

Managing residual symptoms of OCD can be challenging. It takes time and effort and can be emotionally exhausting for everyone involved. What is most important to note is that it may get worse before it gets better.

This may be easiest to understand with an analogy. OCD behaviors are a result of anxious feelings. The OCD brain believes that if your child participates in the behavior, then the anxiety will go away, and they feel better. Think of your child's OCD behaviors as a baby's pacifier. When a baby is crying you give them a pacifier. This makes the baby stop crying. If you take the pacifier away, the baby starts crying again. Often, therefore, to make the baby feel better you give back the pacifier.

Now think about when we try to wean a baby off a pacifier. When we take it away, the baby may cry or act out in some other way. But we don't give the pacifier back, because we want the baby to learn they can survive without it. The crying or tantrum may get worse, but we still don't give it back because we know they will be okay. We are trying to change the behavior. In general, ERP functions in the same way. When you prevent a child from engaging in a compulsive behavior they will likely cry, tantrum, or act out in another way. This may go on for some time. But it is not productive to allow the behavior just to relieve the tantrum. We continue to prevent it, because we know they will be okay; over time, your child's brain will likewise learn they will be okay, even without performing compulsions. Again, this approach is most beneficial when children are stable enough to engage with therapy—placing limits that lead to more tantrums and acting out may not be wise if a child is still in the throes of acute inflammation and the atypical behaviors that follow from it.

If you are able to effectively maintain ERP at home, exposures should get much easier over time. As the child learns they will be okay, they will likely be more responsive to prompting. Tantrums, crying, and acting out will likely decrease. However, the OCD thoughts often take a long time to go away. So as your child starts to manage them better, they may just need gentle reminders along the way.

Conclusion and key points

Once past the acute-onset state, OCD is best managed through close collaboration between parents, medical providers, and a mental health provider. Exposure and response prevention, while increasing your child's distress at first, will eventually help your child to break free of some of the compulsions, rituals, and obsessive thoughts that may have characterized his or her illness. As mentioned previously, do remain in close contact with your medical provider, as a worsening of OCD symptoms can sometimes indicate a physical relapse or exposure to a new illness. In this case, you may work with your therapist to adjust or delay implementation of any new ERP treatment.

In particular, keep the following in mind:

— For children who are physically healthy enough to address OCD symptoms, consistent expectations and processes are key.

— Exposing your child to his or her feared triggers may provoke intense distress, even tantrums, but will eventually help him or her to realize that he or she will be okay and that the underlying fear is not rational.

10

Managing Anxiety on a Daily Basis

Myesha, a 14-year-old with PANS triggered by mycoplasma pneumonia (a bacterial infection commonly known as walking pneumonia), underwent plasmapheresis (a procedure in which improperly functioning plasma cells are filtered out of the bloodstream) and several rounds of IVIG at a local teaching hospital. She experienced immediate improvement in many of her symptoms, including restricted eating, rage, and intense tics. But even after this medical treatment, she continued to have intense anxiety connected with leaving the house or, to a lesser degree, separating from her mother. This fear was particularly intense at nighttime. Myesha's parents considered more immunotherapy, but their neurologist advised them to wait a few months to see if more improvement would occur over the long term as her immune system adjusted. If not, she advised, they could always consider additional intensive treatment. In the meantime, she recommended keeping Myesha as healthy as possible, pursuing therapy for Myesha's anxiety, and continuing efforts to reduce her fear of leaving the house. Myesha's parents had previously been accommodating her anxiety while she was in crisis, but they gradually began to ask her to leave the house with them, require her to spend some time outside her bedroom, and encourage her to face some of her persistent fears. However, this was at times a bumpy road. Myesha's mother confided to her therapist, "I feel like such a bad mom for making her do all these things that she is afraid of!"

While we know OCD can be closely linked to other forms of anxiety, children with PANDAS, PANS, or encephalitis can also present with generalized and separation anxiety. "Generalized Anxiety Disorder (GAD) is characterized by persistent and excessive worry about a number of different things" (Anxiety and Depression Association of America n.d.). Separation anxiety, on the other hand, involves specific fear of "being lost from" family members or having "something bad happening" if separation from family members (or preferred places) occurs (Stanford Children's Health n.d.). Anxiety, particularly separation anxiety, may manifest with a child's being afraid to sleep alone, experiencing excessive fear or concern over something, avoiding situations in which he or she is alone, experiencing somatic symptoms (including headaches or bellyaches), and, at times, acting out when fears and worries are not addressed (Stanford Children's Health n.d.). As we continue to discuss managing these manifestations of anxiety, it is important to keep in mind that a child with PANDAS or PANS may not exhibit all symptoms at all times associated with either generalized or separation anxiety. This is, in part, because of the natural ebb and flow of PANDAS and PANS symptoms.

Constructive (and non-constructive) approaches

As a parent, when we see our child suffering, our first instinct may be to fix it, relieve their distress, and help them feel better. But sometimes, as Myesha's parents realized in the opening vignette, our best intentions can be counterproductive. When someone is suffering from anxiety, their fears and worries feel real, no matter how illogical or impractical they may seem. One way to support a child suffering from an anxiety disorder is by knowing what not to say. Comments that reinforce a child's fear are likely to be ineffective, as are exhortations to calm down, get over their fears, or stop worrying (Rollin 2015). Rather, empathetic listening can be key, validating children's emotions while also helping them move beyond their anxiety. See Box 10.1 for examples of things to say to your child when anxiety symptoms are causing them distress.

Box 10.1: What to say when your child experiences anxiety

- I am here with you until you calm down. Is there something else we can try to focus on in the meantime? What can you see around you? What can you smell? Can you tell me how this [any object] feels to you right now? I have some [preferred food] for you to try. Can you tell me how it tastes? What are some sounds you can hear around you?

- I know this really feels like a big deal for you right now. That is okay. We will work through it until you feel better.

- I can see that this is really difficult for you.

- I know thinking about this happening in the future seems scary for you. Let's talk about what is happening right now. Can you tell me what's happening right now?

- Let's make a list of things you can control in the moment.

Additionally, meditation and deep breathing may be helpful, particularly when children are in the healing phase of illness and have the attention span and stability to engage with these practices. Meditation and deep breathing can take on many forms, depending on your preferences, your child's preferences, any religious or spiritual practices your family already incorporates into day-to-day activities, and resources available to you. You may find helpful guidance on the internet by searching for relaxation, meditation, or deep breathing videos. Increasingly, there are apps which help children or adults focus on deep breathing and relaxation (a search on your device's app store for "deep breathing" or "meditation" should help you identify some). Children and teens, who gravitate toward the convenience of mobile devices, may find these particularly helpful. An added benefit of deep breathing or meditation apps is that they can be accessed anywhere and are available in any setting where your child has his or her device. It is helpful to keep in mind that meditation and deep breathing may require patience and practice over time before your child feels completely comfortable using them, but both can have significant positive results if you invest the time.

Separation anxiety can be particularly challenging and frustrating for children (or adults) with PANDAS, PANS, or AE and for their caregivers. As separation anxiety is a "hallmark symptom" of PANDAS and PANS (Kovacevic n.d.), it is frequently a challenge that caregivers and children confront. Separation anxiety, as described earlier, may manifest with reluctance to leave one's home in general, a preferred location within the home, or a preferred person (such as a parent). Like other residual symptoms, this may be best addressed—as Myesha's family found out in the opening vignette—once more intensive symptoms have been addressed through medical treatment. Once that point is reached, therapies such as cognitive behavioral therapy (CBT) and dialectical behavioral therapy (DBT), both discussed below, can be useful. As a parent or caregiver, it is important to know that helping your child move beyond separation anxiety is likely to involve some temporary distress to him or her as he or she re-establishes comfort levels with new (or rediscovered) places and experiences. Be patient and gentle even when setting expectations for growth ("I know you don't want to leave the house. Today, we are going to go to two different places together: the park and the store, where we will buy your favorite kind of ice cream. I know this may feel scary, but I will be with you and I will be ready to listen and talk about your feelings as you come with me").

Cognitive behavioral therapy, discussed in the preceding chapter, can be helpful as a treatment for anxiety as well. In addition, for those who are not helped by a traditional CBT approach, dialectical behavior therapy may offer some promise. DBT is an evidence-based treatment, grounded in principles of both CBT and mindfulness, developed by psychology researcher and clinician Marsha Linehan (Linehan Institute n.d.). Unlike traditional CBT, which emphasizes changes in thinking patterns and behavior, dialectical therapy aims to help patients synthesize two dialectics, or opposite ideas—in this case, "acceptance" of distressing thoughts or ideas, and "change" in reaction patterns so that they can better address those thoughts or build a meaningful life despite them (Linehan Institute n.d.). Specific skills emphasized in DBT include mindfulness, tolerance of distress, interpersonal effectiveness, and regulation of emotions (Linehan Institute n.d.).

As with other modes of therapy, DBT may be most effective in treating residual symptoms while your child is in the healing phase of his or her illness. You may wish to ask therapists, as you consider working with them, whether they are familiar with DBT and feel comfortable implementing it, particularly if your child does not respond to traditional CBT. If therapy is not a realistic option for you, there are numerous workbooks and at-home resources that may be useful (see Further Reading).

While DBT may be an effective tool for older children, this may be too complicated for a younger child suffering with PANDAS, PANS, or autoimmune encephalitis. It will be important to utilize tools whose language and concepts are more appropriate for younger children in the healing phase.

If you choose to make use of these workbooks, it is recommended you use them with the assistance of your child's therapist. However, if your child is unable to participate in therapy, it is recommended you, as the caregiver, read through the workbooks first to become familiar with the concepts and language. You can, then, effectively introduce them to your child, assist them in working through the concepts, and refer them back to these resources in times of particular distress.

Conclusion and key points

Anxiety is all too familiar for many children and families dealing with PANDAS and PANS. Parents often find there is a balance between offering caring and empathetic support, on the one hand, and reinforcing unreasonable fears, on the other. The resources in this chapter should be helpful in assisting you as you seek that balance. In particular:

— Encourage your child to identify other things to think about or engage with until the episode of anxiety passes.

— Let your child know you love him or her even if you are not discussing the specific anxiety trigger at the moment.

— Seek support for yourself, including peer support or friendship as well as medical and mental health providers.

11

Grieving and Family Relationships

Aaron and Lucia were parents of two children with PANS, whose symptom onset occurred at the same time and took two years to resolve back to a tolerable level. Once both their children were stabilized, Aaron and Lucia expected life to return to normal—or, at least, to a "new normal" that would allow them to move ahead. They were surprised, though, to discover that the opposite seemed to occur. While their children were able to resume their pre-PANS lifestyle, Aaron and Lucia found themselves fighting every day, sometimes to the point of screaming. Neither was sleeping well, and Lucia began having nightmares. One day, when Aaron floated the idea of moving out because of the tension in their relationship, they finally decided to seek couples counseling to try to find a way to move forward.

As Aaron and Lucia found out, sometimes the post-recovery period is the most taxing on relationships, particularly for caregivers. While you may experience intense stress during periods of significant illness, your expectations for productive or enjoyable times with your partner may be much lower as a result of the intensity of your child's illness. In contrast, once your child is stable, you may find yourself struggling to reclaim a sense of normality—one that you may not have experienced for months or even years.

Addressing this challenge often requires us to consider the nature and dimensions of our "new normal," including the current status of a child's symptoms, and then to reassess the impact of those current symptoms on our other relationships—especially with a partner. Some suggestions for doing so follow.

Confronting your new normal

As you help your child navigate through the healing phase of their illness, it is important to continue to revisit your new normal. As they continue to heal, your normal will continue to change. This is a good time for you to take a self-inventory on what you should and can expect from your child, your family, and yourself. Good questions to ask yourself could include:

- *What were my child's symptoms when we started?* Take an inventory of the symptoms your child experienced in the acute stage of their illness. Determine which symptoms have subsided. Be mindful of age-appropriate negative behaviors as well. For example, a six-year-old with and without AE can experience tantrums. Try to navigate between what is a symptom of illness and what is an age-appropriate behavior.

- *What are my child's current symptoms?* What are the current residual symptoms your child is struggling with? Is it age-appropriate behavior? Are there ways you are able to tell the difference? Make sure not to focus on symptoms which were relieved in the course of appropriate medical treatment. For example, if your child struggled to sleep alone when in the acute phase, but is now sleeping alone well, do not address this symptom in fear that it may return. Only focus on current symptoms.

- *Are my expectations too high or too low based on their stage of illness?* Make sure you are setting standards based on what your child is capable of. If your initial expectation of your child was to get all As in school but they are now managing Cs with effort, then change your expectation to what they are capable of. At the same time, make sure you are challenging your child to get better. Make sure not to accept Cs if they are putting in little effort and they are capable of more. You will need to pay attention to where you child is at in their recovery to make sure you are not pushing too hard but also not enabling old behaviors.

- *Can I/should I adjust how I parent at this time?* It's important to remember that how you parented your child before illness may not be the same as how you parent during the acute and healing phases of the illness. In addition to this, be mindful of how you may not be able to have the same expectation of your child with PANDAS or PANS as you do your other children without PANDAS or PANS. Ultimately, all children are different. Noticing what each child needs from you and when they need it is something that will come from personal insight and self-reflection.

- *Am I continuing to do the same things but expecting different results?* Is what you are doing working? If not, try to mix it up a little. The reality is that sometimes nothing you do will work. The illness will be stronger. However, when your child is in recovery, it will be important to ask yourself this question many times throughout the process. If you know what is not working, try something new.

- *Is fear of relapse running our lives?* If you are walking on egg shells worried about a relapse, your child will likely struggle to get better. If we help them to avoid uncomfortable situations, we are enabling anxiety and/or OCD. Unfortunately, part of our job in the healing phase is to help our child face what is uncomfortable. If they are forced to experience uncomfortable situations, they will also learn they can get through them. Under most circumstances, their discomfort equals your discomfort. But you, too, will get through. The best way to navigate uncomfortable symptoms is to face them, work through them, and then realize that you are all still okay.

Managing relationships with your partner

There is no doubt that having a child with special needs can take a toll on your relationship with your partner. When we decide to spend our lives with someone and plan a family we do not envision it with a child with special needs. We don't anticipate the stress that comes with caring for a child who is ill. And we can't anticipate the impact that this will have on our partnership.

Communication

Even under the healthiest of circumstances, parents often have differ-ent parenting styles and can struggle with not being on the same page.

This may be an extra challenge for your family as you navigate through your child's illness. You and your partner do not need to always agree on how to parent. However, there needs to be communication about how to manage different symptoms. One parent may be more equipped to manage different circumstances. Discussing a plan for tag-teaming will be helpful. Also, discuss with your partner how to identify symptoms of burnout, which may manifest differently for each of you. As you notice your partner exhibiting signs of burnout or stress, you can implement your tag-team plan to give each other a rest when it is most needed. It is best to engage in these conversations when your child is not in crisis, rather than trying to develop a plan while simultaneously coping with crisis.

Making time for your relationship

Your child's illness does not define your relationship. Taking time for your relationship, away from the children, will help you to remember you are a partnership. This can be as simple as taking a walk around the block together, a short coffee date, working out together, or checking in at night after the kids are in bed. While some of this time may need to be utilized to check in on managing your child's illness, it will also be important to make sure some of your quality time does not include discussing the children. Take time to connect. If you do not have access to child care or cannot leave your child with a sitter, go sit on the porch for ten minutes together—be flexible. It is helpful, too, in extremely stressful times, to keep your expectations realistic for time together. You may both be in a heightened state of anxiety yourselves, and having the perfect date night may be unrealistic; in these cases, take some time to sit together, touch or hold hands, breathe together, and even be silent together.

Creating a support system

Ask for help! You cannot do this alone. Reach out to those around you who are supportive and let them help you. Family may or may not be a source of support. Due to the controversial nature of the illness, many friends and family members may not believe in the illness. It is important to be prepared for family and friends to not be supportive. Don't spend your time trying to convince these people of the illness.

When your child is sick, you will need to surround yourself with people who can listen and help. Engaging with family or friends who dispute the illness will only hinder your well-being. Surround yourself with people who are healthy for you.

Support groups are all over the United States and the world. It is common for people to seek out support online as it allows people to connect without having to leave their child or their home. You can use Google to find local support groups and/or Facebook for public and/or private support groups. While using the internet to connect is valuable, attending support groups in person can have the added benefit of personal connection. It also gives you some time out of the home and allows you to work on self-care.

Seeking therapy

Yes, it's hard to find time to attend therapy once per week. But what if it can truly help you manage this illness better? Parents of children with mental and physical illness are (naturally and understandably) not equipped with the tools or information to best manage rare diseases with disruptive and sometimes destructive symptoms. In fact, there is no way to prepare for the emotional and physical toll this will take on a parent. Therapy can offer education about how to better manage your child's illness. Additionally, therapy can help you to better manage the emotional stress that the illness has caused for you. If you and your partner are struggling to manage the illness together, seek out couples therapy and/or coaching. This can help you to improve on parenting skills. Once you are on the same page, together you can help your child heal and manage the residual mental health symptoms they are suffering with.

Grieving the loss of your living child

Yes, you read that correctly. Likely, you are grieving the loss of your living child. More accurately, you are experiencing ambiguous grief, defined as "times in life when someone we love becomes someone we barely recognize…is still physically with us, but psychologically… gone" (Williams 2017). These feelings may manifest in a range of different ways, with depression, anger or rage, sadness, or regret. You may feel guilt (Williams 2017) over steps you did take, didn't take, or imagined taking. Ambiguous grief can be particularly difficult to deal with because we may not recognize our feelings as being related to grief, and others—those who might be the first to provide support in the event of a death—likewise may not realize we are grieving. In reality, this type of grief is not terribly different from the grief we may feel upon an actual death. Many parents of children with PANDAS or PANS encounter sudden loss of their child, who one day is happy and healthy and the next day is gone. In fact, your emotions may be even more conflicted because, in addition to grieving the child who has disappeared, you are constantly challenged by learning to parent this new person with new behaviors, emotions, and responses.

Once you allow yourself self-compassion and permission to grieve, there are ways to try to navigate through that grieving process. It can be helpful to hold on to prior memories, even as you also try to move on. Remember, also, that the symptoms of illness should not define your entire response to your child—he or she is a person underneath those symptoms and independent of them (Williams 2017). This is especially important to remember when your child is suffering from AE as there will be relapses and remissions in the illness. Allow yourself to embrace the healing phase (making positive memories as you experience more positive outcomes), and then separate the illness from the child during flares.

Additionally, be willing to acknowledge the pain you are feeling rather than pretending it doesn't exist. It may be helpful to connect with others experiencing similar pain, as they can relate to you and provide support. There are numerous national, regional, and local support groups available through social media, through the PANDAS Network support group pages,[1] and other venues (PANDAS-aware physicians and therapists may also maintain a list of such groups locally).

Conclusion and key points

It is normal to feel grief—and the stages of grief, including anger, sadness, and frustration—when experiencing the ups and downs of PANDAS or PANS. Sometimes, the stress of this process can be compounded, in fact, by the nature of this particular illness, which does not follow a stable path for many children and families. Parents, partners, and siblings experiencing grief and other complex

---

1   www.pandasnetwork.org

emotional responses to a family member's illness might do well to remember the following:

- Be kind to yourself in the midst of this stress and emotional adjustment; acknowledge your grief, anger, and frustration.

- Don't be afraid to look back on positive experiences or good times and believe that you will experience such times again.

- Seek out comfort and support from others experiencing similar issues, whether online or in person.

12

Family Self-Care

ACKNOWLEDGING TRAUMA

Jamie and Jerome were parents of Ellie, a four-year-old whose PANDAS onset that year had been sudden and terrifying for all concerned. Ellie underwent two psychiatric hospitalizations and was diagnosed with childhood schizophrenia before she received a correct PANDAS diagnosis from a local psychiatrist, who immediately referred Jamie and Jerome to a university clinic two hours away for further evaluation and treatment. At the university clinic, Ellie was treated with plasmapheresis, requiring another inpatient stay, and then several rounds of outpatient IVIG. Her team of specialists discussed options in case she did not respond, including rituximab. Jerome felt weak in the stomach just looking at the list of side effects.

On their way out of the clinic, both Jamie and Jerome were shell-shocked, and they continued to feel that way even as Ellie slowly, almost imperceptibly, improved. Four months later, she had finally progressed to the point that they could leave her with a sitter and go out to dinner. When they arrived at the restaurant, though, Jerome was unable to relax. He paced, fidgeted, and breathed deeply, attempting to calm himself for this long-awaited date night. "What's the matter with you?" Jamie said, looking at him. "Calm down! She's finally getting better. You don't even have anything to be upset about anymore!"

Nearly every family that encounters PANDAS or PANS has to confront trauma, and post-traumatic stress, at some point. This illness is uniquely disruptive and even terrifying for families. In this and the following chapter, we share reflections from a personal, rather than a clinical, perspective. Diana Pohlman, founder of the PANDAS Network, has worked with thousands of families who have experienced these traumatic events, and in these two chapters, she shares her own experience, captures some of the emerging research around parent and caregiver stress, and provides words of advice from her perspective as both advocate and parent.

I write as a lay person, mother, caregiver of two PANDAS children; I may not address everyone's experiences in this reflection but hope to share my own insight for others' benefit. I asked my daughter (age 14), "Tell me something to give me courage to write this." And she replied, "You have to prepare people so they can not worry so much. If they know this is what PANDAS does, they will be more confident as their child heals." I cannot fix everyone's heartache here—but I can tell you: You are not alone. Do not walk this path alone. Community support is essential.

Additionally, those in support services (therapists, counselors, physicians) must realize the impact of PANDAS and PANS on families and the stress and isolation they feel during the course of the illness, especially the acute phase. As a result of this stress, the entire family needs attention. As we wait for research to unfold, there is still an urgent need to pay attention to the effects of these illnesses on the family system. Families dealing with PANDAS, PANS, or autoimmune encephalitis need help transitioning from sickness to well-being and health in a measured, compassionate way.

What families report

The research cited here talks about young patients between the ages of 4 and 18. Increasingly, we are seeing that adolescents and young adults are susceptible to PANDAS. These young persons need another tool kit of care and education that we have yet to develop. While young adults are not addressed in the current research, you might consider how these findings might also apply to a young adult, living semi-independently or on their own.

Families dealing with PANDAS, PANS, or autoimmune encephalitis often experience isolation, fatigue, confusion, and depression, especially in the acute onset phase of the illness. Some children (and their families) who have more unstable courses of healing need even more attention and compassion. A recent study conducted by nurses and nurse practitioners reported on the quality of life and emotional perceptions of families dealing with PANDAS and PANS. They found three main themes repeating in families' experiences: fear, frustration, and not being heard (McClelland *et al.* 2015). These findings speak to the isolation families feel and the importance of having medical professionals, particularly nurses and nursing educators, collaborate to assist and support families (McClelland *et al.* 2015).

My suggestions for supporting families are provided below, born of personal experience as a parent and professional working with thousands of families touched by this disease.

- *Communication*: Sharing information about chronic illness can lessen fear on the part of families. Professionals can share new developments in research and treatment plans; children can be provided playtime, favorite blankets, or even a visit from a friend at times of procedures.

- *Listening and hearing families' stories*: Improved compassion and caring leads to a lessening of stress and to a sense of well-being. There is often tension in the corporate medical system of delivery and parents need to be aware of this; find at least one heartfelt practitioner in a team you may employ (for example, a nurse, pediatrician, counselor, nutritionist) to be that caring ear you need.

- *Working together with frontline nurses, schools, and other practitioners*: Evidence-based practices are slow to develop during the period of uncertainty while the disease model is still being understood. It is essential to persist and advocate with other parents; often, among families dealing with PANDAS and PANS, progress for one family can offer a sense of inspiration or accomplishment to others in the community.

Caregiver burden

A study conducted by the Stanford PANS Clinic used the Caregiver Burden Index (CBI) to measure caregiver burden, a measure of stress, fatigue, and difficulty for care providers, for over one hundred caregivers during their children's active PANS flare. The CBI, a well-validated study in adult populations, measured five specific areas of well-being for caregivers: "time dependency, emotional health, physical health, development, and social relationships" (Farmer *et al.* 2018, p.750). The CBI of caring for children with PANS (including PANDAS) was greater than that of caring for Alzheimer's patients (Farmer *et al.* 2018).

In other words, if parents or caregivers feel that caring for a child with PANDAS or PANS is extraordinarily stressful, they are correct. Consider the necessity of building in supports during this illness and accepting, temporarily, a slower pace of life in managing an ill child. Unfortunately, respite care for families of children with PANDAS or PANS is not yet readily available or covered by insurance, though efforts must be made to change this.

In this study, the greatest toll reported on families was the sense of isolation and disconnection from normal life (Farmer *et al.* 2018). It is important for families to monitor these specific areas of burden. Monitor the hours of caregiving; be mindful of depression and social isolation. Be mindful, also, of your own lack of choice in being a caregiver and acknowledge your feelings about that situation honestly. Being honest about your feelings does not mean you love your child any less; on the contrary, it means you love them enough to be honest about what you need in order to continue to care for them. Talk to someone you love earnestly about needing a break, even if it is to walk down the street or run to the store alone. Try to find respite even if for an hour a day.

Truly, it does help to talk and communicate with support groups (online or in person) and, if you can afford it, to seek counseling for yourself and your family. If you cannot sleep or you become depressed or anxious, see a medical professional who can help you assess whether pharmacologic interventions are needed and would be helpful. In my experience working with children and families, the first few months of diagnosis and treatment are often the most difficult, as symptoms may diminish gradually and as you adjust to your own "new normal," discussed elsewhere in this book.

Self-harm: Difficult discussions about a difficult topic

Impulses toward self-harm can be a topic difficult to discuss but truly important to acknowledge and address. In one study of children with pediatric OCD (Storch *et al.* 2015), the following significant issues occurred. Please take the list of symptoms below seriously and create an intervention plan, when indicated, that addresses aspects of self-harm.

More than half of all participants (51%) scored in the clinically significant range for thought problems, including seeing or hearing things and thoughts or actions focused on harming themselves. For participants between the ages of 6 and 18, nearly one third (30%) indicated suicidal responses on the checklist used to assess their state of mind, including "talks about killing self" and/or "deliberately harms self or attempts suicide" (Storch *et al.* 2015).

Suicidal thoughts and ideation are complicated topics—they change with age, intensity of depression, and levels of expressed hopelessness. For families dealing with PANDAS or PANS, it is important not to hide OCD, but rather to talk about it openly and really teach the child that their immune system is "tricking their brain." With severe OCD, learning to "talk back to the OCD brain" is strongly recommended. There are very good tools created by psychiatrists used within CBT or other forms of psychiatric care, referenced earlier in this book.

It is not unusual with acute onset to hear your child saying things about wanting to die or engage in self-harm. It is shocking, and even terrifying, as a parent to hear your child say these things. It is essential, as a parent, to share this information immediately with your child's doctor, including care providers such as your counselor, psychiatrist, and neurologist. Understand that this is also a function of illness—but, like any other aspect of illness, it must be addressed rapidly and proactively, with appropriate medical attention.

Please know that healing a child of PANDAS-induced OCD is something that can be done—even if a child manifests suicidal ideation. As the caregiver, share your fears with your own support persons (clergy, friends, counselor, etc.). Lean on your online community: vent, cry, talk, make mistakes in how you state things! It's okay—just keep talking and talking and find the path out. The PANDAS community will continue to grow and support you.

13

Moving Beyond Trauma

"These children have had their childhood ripped away. They face hardships that would bring a grown man to his knees, but they are warriors. Our children deserve more than this."

Anonymous PANS mom

The goal of this chapter is to explain how difficult it has been for many parents or caregivers to recover from the experience of encountering PANDAS or PANS. It is important to appreciate this, not in order to discourage parents just beginning this journey, but to provide encouragement that even in the midst of a long and arduous process, there is hope and, again, you are not alone. It is normal to take time to recover, and normal to feel the effects of trauma and stress.

PANDAS or PANS is most often disorienting and traumatic initially but as healing begins (and it does), recovery can be transformative in a deeply personal and positive way. The online community of families and various activist groups around the world are helping relieve some of the burden of the journey for newly diagnosed families.

Post-traumatic stress disorder (PTSD) is defined as a disorder that "develops in some people who have experienced a shocking, scary or dangerous event" (NIMH 2016). Symptoms of PTSD can arise within a varying timeframe after the event, but must be present consistently for at least a month in order for an individual to be diagnosed with PTSD. Typically, adults diagnosed with PTSD will have at least one "re-experiencing" symptom (such as flashbacks or nightmares) connected with the traumatic event, one "avoidance" symptom (trying to stay away from places, events, or memories connected with the event), at least two "arousal and reactivity" symptoms (feeling tense, feeling nervous or on edge, having outbursts), and at least two "mood and cognition" symptoms (trouble remembering, negative thoughts, feelings of guilt or blame, and depressive feelings) (NIMH 2016). These symptoms may also manifest in children, though children may also experience additional responses including bedwetting, re-enacting the event in playtime, or exhibiting unusual anxiety or clingy behavior. (It is worth noting that these symptoms can also overlap with those of PANDAS or PANS.)

It is not unusual for parents and caregivers of children with PANDAS or PANS to experience symptoms of PTSD. Indeed, the difficulties of diagnosis, managing complex behaviors, potentially hospitalizing children, and facing sometimes-devastating financial consequences can all create significant trauma and stress for family members.

When confronted with a PANDAS or PANS diagnosis, even the most grounded person is bewildered and shocked. It is breath-stopping to watch your pride and joy, your child, transformed and tormented while you are unable to stop it. As you watch the child change overnight, as a parent, it can feel like your very DNA has changed and your life turns inside out. Speaking from personal experience and from my experience counseling hundreds of families, I can say that in initial phases of illness, there is often misunderstanding of all kinds: mother to child, mother to father, friend to friend, teacher to child, teacher to parent, doctor to parent, sibling to sibling. In addition, there often is isolation, fear and anger, loneliness, retreating from friends or spouse, and impact on work. It is challenging to rest or relax, and your child's sudden, disruptive symptoms mean that you are typically hyperfocused on them. In a 2018 survey conducted by PANDAS Network, over 70 percent of parents said their child presented with all or nearly all of the following symptoms at onset: OCD, tics, separation anxiety, irritability, concentration issues, hyperactivity, developmental regression, and sleep issues. Additionally, over 70 percent of parents said the illness impacted their child's ability to perform normal, day-to-day activities such as attending school (PANDAS Network 2018). Considering the extent of this impact, it is not surprising that parents respond in the ways described above.

What are initial reactions to this explosion of change? Parents might spank or scold or yell in the first week or days of these symptoms. Parents of older children might underestimate the importance of the teen's or young adult's feelings of anxiety or OCD or lack of sleep. There is pressure from everyone to keep things going as expected: school, work, schedules, friendships, fun times, affection—but these areas may change instantly, sometimes gradually.

As time goes on, these initial reactions might solidify into a form of hypervigilance, as parents are constantly anticipating difficulty. Parents take on roles as advocates, therapists, and sometimes medical consultants, adding to their stress. Additional areas of impact in this phase may include lost time (searching for therapists and educational consultants or new school placements), stress in searching for care providers and respite care, and out-of-pocket medical costs. In the 2018 PANDAS Network survey, 30 percent of parents reported spending between $5000 and $20,000 out of pocket on their child's illness.

At this point, as the child stabilizes, parents may regain a sense of order and control. However, the intense energy required to cope with onset and maintenance can continue to impact one psychologically for years and years. At this point, it is truly helpful to have the support of a community that understands PANDAS, PANS, and their impact on families.

I will give one simple personal example of hypervigilance and ongoing, post-traumatic impact. Before PANDAS, I used to love listening to music at all times in my home, and had grown up with many kinds of music surrounding me. When my child became ill, I stopped playing music because I needed to focus on his issues to keep him safe. I stopped listening to music—at all. I could not listen to it for several years because I was sure I would miss something my child needed; he might get sick and I had to be ready and focused; music would distract me.

In many domains of a person's life, this hypervigilance, disassociation from joy, or difficulty returning to your previous identity may occur at moments that you least expect: getting back to school, going to the office back to work, visiting friends, watching TV, going for a walk—the list is endless. And in my experience and that of families I've counseled, this can make us feel many different emotions: anger, sadness, fear, courage, weakness, loneliness, or desparation. It is, once again, a new path; take it slow and get to know yourself in a new way. In my experience, the path to recovery is a tricky balance—period. Each person recovers at their own rate but the main point is to re-enter life as slowly as possible for an easy transition. When you see that your child needs you less and is indeed healing there is a wonderful feeling of exaltation and relief. You will probably feel stronger and proud of yourselves and your child. There is often a very real change in your awareness of life and how you relate to others.

Parents report that life feels different because they understand that simplicity and joy can be changed with a finger-snap and that well-meaning professionals can leave us feeling abandoned and ignored. We know what it is like to feel unprotected. There is not enough space here to acknowledge the depth of despair and anger many of us have felt. We have gone into places of fear and loss that have come about in a manner unique to PANDAS and PANS. We have now entered that arena of "survivors of…" and we have a wholly new view of life.

Survivors crawl out of their survival mode when the coast seems clear enough, manageable. Rejoining life is a natural and necessary process. And if it is difficult to do so, there are many who have gone before us. One of the most powerful ways to come out of "the jail of trauma" is to develop an acceptance that life is constantly re-creating and changeable. Below, I describe a few steps that were helpful to me in developing this acceptance of life's changes.

First step: Forgiveness

There can be a great deal of anger and regret felt over the chaos PANDAS and PANS inflicted on our lives. Churning thoughts of anger, guilt, and exhaustion often overshadow the early days of recovery. You may blame yourself, your child, your medical team, or others for the onset or progression of your child's illness. But don't stop there. True healing may come when we accept the world as it is, with its pain and imperfection (Kushner 2004), even when we cannot change it.

Second step: Letting go of the old view of life

As the child heals and finances are reworked, marriage dynamics are re-evaluated and re-established, and routine returns, most parents have told me they "don't feel the same" in their relationships. Life feels different—disconnected. Christina Rasmussen describes the transition of emerging from trauma:

> I like to call this space the Waiting Room. When we're in the Waiting Room, we're still attached to the past… We struggle with our new reality, thinking that is our new life… [Our] ability to plan and reason

is temporarily gone… Then we begin to experiment with our new life. This is perhaps the scariest aspect of life after loss, because so much is unknown and has to be taken on faith. (Rasmussen 2013, p.25)

This process of experimentation and transformation requires us to look gently at our new emotions, reactions, and behaviors and those of others around us. As you emerge into this phase, continue to seek support, but remember also that there is a life beyond PANDAS and PANS, and be careful of how much time you spend (online, in particular) exploring resources when you may find fulfillment in re-engaging with the world beyond PANS.

Third step: Feel the fear and do it anyway

It is important to know that the vast majority of these children heal entirely. Letting go of the safety net of fear and self-protection is a process, as we realize children are on the path to healing, and it will occur differently for each of us. Rasmussen (2013) suggests focusing on discrete "plug-in" activities to help you focus and re-center. She suggests finding the one area of your life you find most frustrating and take the smallest step to move, slowly, toward resolving that and practice taking 15 minutes out of each day to work on that area. For example, if you have felt stuck in your home and unable to enjoy life much, a "plug-in" might be to take a new street, stop at a new coffee shop or store you have never seen before, or go to a bookstore or library and spend a few minutes looking through new books. Remember that fulfillment doesn't mean absence of pain or regret.

Researcher Brené Brown has spent years quantifying what helps people to have courage, vulnerability, shame, and empathy. Spirituality, she found, plays an important role, without necessarily requiring religion, theology, or doctrine:

> Spirituality is recognizing and celebrating that we are all inextricably connected to one another by a power greater than all of us, and that our connection to that power and to one another is grounded in love and belonging. Our expressions of spirituality are as diverse as we are. When our intentions and actions are guided by spirituality—the belief in our interconnectedness and love—our everyday experiences can be spiritual practices. (Brown 2017, pp.10–11)

Spirituality, meditation, and reflection can be critical elements in our recovery and journey to wholeness, whatever shape or form that might take for each of us.

This—resilience, spirituality, grace, forgiveness—is what you parents have built from this trauma, grief, and pain. As you reconstruct your life after the difficulty and trauma of a PANDAS or PANS onset, know that it will go on. Your child will recover and you may find that, as that occurs, you are able to spread awareness and support to others as well. This is what the few courageous researchers and physicians are working with us on. It has become our mission and task on this earth. We are changing the world.

3

Planning, Advocacy, and Communication

14

Routines, Supports, and Social Skills

Glen, a dad of three, sometimes reflects on his life B.P. (before PANS) and A.P. (after PANS). Before ten-year-old son Bobby, his third child, was diagnosed with PANS, the family kept to a strict routine: school, homework, karate practice, healthy dinner, half hour of computer games, and bedtime before nine for everyone. Even more than the kids, Glen and his wife Michelle thrived on the peace and quiet of their routine. After Bobby's PANDAS symptoms began, though, Glen felt the entire house had been turned upside down. Even as Bobby began treatment and improved, it was difficult to get back into routine. Both Glen and Michelle continued to feel on edge, and their other children needed therapy as well to cope with the stress of Bobby's illness. Glen wondered if he would ever be able to get back to his original routine.

Frequently, families facing PANDAS and PANS have reported to us that even after their children have stabilized from the initial crisis phase, they experience difficulty returning to their prior routines. This difficulty may stem from several factors: families whose children experience PANDAS or PANS find their financial circumstances and schedules may change dramatically; children whose health status has been altered may end up changing schools, activities, and even friends, causing more disruption in routine. Also, family members, along with children themselves, may experience post-traumatic stress symptoms which can make it challenging to carry out familiar routines. This chapter addresses some common issues related to disruption in routines and provides some suggestions for families as they work to establish a "new normal."

PANDAS/PANS: Impact on routines

Disruption in routines may result during the initial illness, when a child's symptoms begin and require substantial adjustment and accommodation on the part of the family. Routines may also be disrupted as a child stabilizes but requires increased attention from one or both parents to maintain this stability. Last, as a child moves toward recovery, new routines may replace the old ones. These may include substituting homeschooling for traditional school, allergen-free or organic food regimens for more typical ones, or integrating therapist visits into the weekly schedule. In making decisions about new routines, the interests and needs of child and family must be taken into account.

Box 14.1 illustrates how routines may change as children work through, and recover from, effects of illness from PANDAS or PANS.

Box 14.1: Carson's schedule

Carson loved to play basketball. He would get home from fourth grade, have a snack, shoot around in his driveway, and not come in till dinnertime. After dinner, if it was still light, he would return for some more hoops before starting his homework. Being academically gifted, he could get through his homework in about 20 minutes most nights. However, once Carson started showing symptoms of PANS, this routine changed dramatically. Some days, his OCD was so intense that he could not go outside for fear of being kidnapped by a passing stranger. When his OCD finally waned, he found his basketball skills had declined greatly. Suddenly, the thing he had loved most, basketball, was the source of additional distress. Carson's parents gradually found ways to help him hone his rusty basketball skills through fun games, often at the local gym (inside, away from passing cars) or with an older high-school student in the neighborhood whom Carson idolized. Only after six months of treatment and therapy could Carson return to his old routine of happily shooting around, in his driveway, for hours on end.

Evaluating impact on functioning

Setting realistic goals

One important aspect of re-adjusting, for families and for children recovering from PANDAS or PANS, is setting realistic goals. As recovery is gradual and may take an uneven trajectory (NIMH n.d.), this may mean that previously easy tasks become significant goals, and that families accept accomplishing them may take time. For example, Levi, a fourth grader, previously had no difficulty coming home after school and completing homework on his own. After onset of PANS symptoms and multiple rounds of IVIG, Levi finally experienced a significant resolution of most symptoms. However, even after symptoms resolved, he found it impossible to focus on homework for more than ten minutes at a time. Working with his therapist, Levi's family devised a gradual plan to reorient him to these routines as his brain continued to heal. At first, Levi's goal was to come home and (with his grandmother organizing his materials for him) work for ten minutes. Throughout his fifth-grade year, his family gradually lengthened this goal, adjusting for relapses and minor exacerbations; by the end of fifth grade, Levi could finally come home and work independently to complete all his homework. But it took time, patience, and collaborative planning between his family, his therapist, and Levi himself.

Re-establishing family routines

As part of setting realistic goals, it may be helpful (working with your partner, other family members, and/or any therapists who are part of your family's care team) to select one family routine to focus on at a time. Keep in mind, too, that your post-PANDAS routine may end up being quite different from your pre-PANDAS one. For example, if your child's OCD flares in the early evening, moving the time of your family dinner up an hour may make sense—or even skipping family dinner entirely in favor of a brief conversation about the day after school or at bedtime. With all of these decisions, understand that trial and error are essential ways of learning what works for your family—and understand that what works is likely to change from month to month as the trajectory of illness changes as well.

Building social skills

In particular, students may need sustained and repeated practice with social skills in order to regain skills that were lost or that were missed in developmental sequence during extended periods of illness.

Finding and utilizing supports

Families may find sources of support in many places; some of the most common supports are discussed briefly below.

Home

For many families, it can be critical to leverage the internal (within-family) and external (outside the family) supports available as you re-adjust during and after treatment, form new routines, and rebuild lost skills. While family members themselves may be experiencing some forms of post-traumatic reaction following illness (Rice Doran and O'Hanlon 2015), it can be helpful to leverage skills and strengths of family members who can help your child with PANDAS/PANS re-establish some of those previous routines. This may include older siblings, grandparents, parents, and other relatives. It may be helpful to have your family members take stock of their own needs and strengths in order to come up with a plan to address them. See Table 14.1 for an example of the goals chart Yolanda had her children—including Eric, 13, who has PANDAS, and Sophie, 11, who does not—complete as she re-established their home and school routines following a difficult year.

Table 14.1: Goals chart

Goal	What will be easy about this	What will be hard about this	How Mom can help
Get up for school in the morning (Eric)	My alarm is loud	If I am sick or worried it is hard to get up	Remind me of my strategies; come into my room to make sure I'm up
Finish homework in the afternoon (Sophie)	I like to get my homework out of the way	If Eric is having a tantrum about something	Help me get a quiet space to work away from Eric

As evidenced in the chart entries Eric and Sophie filled out, maintaining a routine can be made much easier if family members identify potential challenges, and strategies to address them, well ahead of time.

External supports are important for family members as well. These may include teachers, community members, therapists, and networks of friends; these are discussed below.

School

Additional chapters in this book address school supports in detail. However, in this chapter it is helpful to review, briefly, the importance of communication and coordination with school staff as you re-establish routines, build or rebuild new skills, and generally get back "in the swing of things." In particular, you may wish to talk with school staff about the transition into a new school year (or a new placement) or any other changes which may impact your child's or family's functioning. You'll also want to share with school staff any medical situations which might impact your family's functioning, so that they can work with you to adjust schedules and plans as needed.

Last, if your child is in recovery from PANDAS/PANS, or still experiencing active symptoms, it can be helpful to remind school staff that skills—including social and behavioral skills—may take months or years to return and may return unevenly, in fits and starts rather than according to a consistent trajectory. In particular, take some time to discuss questions such as the following:

- What kind of flexibility is there in attendance policies? Who is the point person for me to communicate with when my child's attendance will be impacted?

- Who is available to help my child establish consistent routines for drop-off, pick-up, lunch, and other potentially stressful times? Will that person understand that PANDAS/PANS sometimes requires flexibility or willingness to adapt existing routines and procedures during acute illness?

- My child is still acquiring the following social skills:

  _____. Is there a staff member available in the school to support him/her in acquiring and using these skills?

- Because my child is still acquiring the following skills:

  _____, he/she may require flexibility in behavioral expectations and classroom procedures. What is the best way for us to communicate about this issue now and in the future?

The example of Evangeline, which follows, provides an illustration of how school staff can support the development of new and constructive routines or help students transition back to previous ones.

Evangeline, eight years old, was a model student for most of second grade. When she contracted strep throat in March of that year, her behavior changed dramatically, and she became unable to complete homework or classwork and unable to participate in recess or gym. She was intensely afraid of germs, dirt, and exposure to other children. As a result, she would frequently demonstrate disruptive behaviors when she felt she was exposed to germs or dirt (including close physical proximity to classmates). Over the summer, with treatment for PANDAS, Evangeline's functioning improved significantly. When she returned to third grade, though, she was still not able to interact successfully with peers, and she still engaged in tantrums when exposed to dirt or sources of potential germs. Over time, these tantrums lessened—but a key ingredient in her improvement was the presence of a supportive third-grade teacher and an understanding behavior interventionist at school. They created an interim behavior plan for Evangeline that spelled out necessary steps and supports during periods of recovery or exacerbation, and they met monthly to evaluate her progress, adjust the plan, and determine when it was appropriate to increase expectations for her to engage in typical classroom interaction.

Community

Supports within the community may include teachers and school staff, therapists, medical care teams, community organizations, your child's previous or current sports teams, or friends. While the availability of these supports may vary, you should not feel shy about approaching community contacts for help and support. Many of the strategies described above for school staff may also be helpful for community members, including leadership in organizations and on sports teams. Explaining your child's specific illness, history, and current needs, along with a description of his or her current routine, can allow community organization leaders to best support your child. In these contexts, it can be useful to know which organizations are subject to federal or state anti-discrimination provisions; it is common for youth sports and youth involvement groups to follow federal guidelines for accessibility and disability discrimination. Knowing this as your child joins or rejoins a group can provide you some confidence in navigating your child's participation within that group.

Conclusion and key points

Re-establishing routines and supporting your child in developing—or redeveloping—appropriate social skills can be challenging. Seeking professional help when necessary and communicating expectations and status changes to school and other professionals who support your child can help to mitigate the challenges outlined in this chapter. Above all, remember that re-establishing your "new normal" after PANDAS or PANS is a lengthy, time-consuming and uneven process—you will have good days and bad days, and both are to be expected.

Some specific strategies that may help are listed below:

— Communicate expectations to your family.

— Be gentle with yourself—ease back into routines when necessary, rather than feeling you must change everything all at once.

— Re-evaluate often and accept that routines that worked well before PANDAS onset may need to be adjusted or even abandoned in this new phase of coping and adjustment.

15

Communicating and Advocating Effectively on Your Child's Behalf

Nina described herself often to friends as "just a mom." She didn't mean that as a putdown or denigration of what she did each day, but as the mother of three small children, she felt that caregiving occupied most of her focus and she was happy with that fact for the time being. She built strong informal connections in her community with other moms, but she had put off ideas of going back to school or back to work until her children grew a bit. Everything changed, though, when her middle child, Casey, was diagnosed with PANS. Horrified by the gaps she saw in the medical and mental health systems and galvanized by the struggles she saw other parents experiencing, she began meeting with her state representative to share the problems she saw and discuss possible solutions. She also connected with other parents through social media, and before she knew it, she had been elected president of a newly formed regional awareness organization for PANDAS, PANS, and autoimmune encephalitis. In order to keep the organization on track to meet its goals—which were ambitious—Nina found herself researching not only legislative advocacy and lobbying but also fundraising. Her husband walked into her makeshift home office one night and, seeing her surrounded by graphs, charts, and policy briefs, joked, "I didn't realize I married a nonprofit CEO!"

There has been a grass roots "warrior mothers" (or "warrior parents") movement of fearless parents leading the advocacy efforts to increase awareness and acceptance of these disorders. These trailblazers are often leading awareness in their prospective career fields or, alternatively, raising awareness from their expert perspective as parents. They are successfully authoring books, facilitating social media sites, establishing and directing statewide as well as national nonprofits, raising large funds for lifesaving treatments, leading community support groups, organizing professional presentations and medical conferences, arranging media coverage, initiating outreach and education to medical providers and beyond. These parents have often been ahead of the science and have organized game-changing interventions, including successful lobbying of legislative bodies for the establishment of PANS medical advisory boards in numerous states. In 2017, mothers associated with PANDAS/PANS Advocacy and Support, a nonprofit in Illinois, spearheaded the passing of a law mandating medical insurance providers to cover necessary treatment, making that state the first in the country to ensure access to treatment. This same nonprofit raises treatment funds to grant to families across the nation several times per year. All these activities constitute examples of advocacy. And yet advocacy can also occur on a much smaller scale; we advocate for our children when we explain their needs to the youth pastor or Little League coach and ask for positive change to facilitate their success.

In some ways, even, this chapter may seem superfluous. Many parents of children with PANDAS or PANS, or related conditions, are well accustomed to advocating for their child and for broader issues related to disease awareness. Often, children receive the correct diagnosis after seeing multiple specialists and receiving several incorrect diagnoses (PANDAS Network 2018); parents often report needing to engage in forceful advocacy with schools or other entities to secure appropriate accommodations so that their child can succeed (Rice Doran and O'Hanlon 2015). One parent of several PANDAS children commented about this chapter's topic, "Advocacy's fine, but I'll be excited when we don't need to advocate anymore!"

Given the reality that advocacy—for one's own child and for the broader disease community—may remain a constant need, this chapter will address strategies for effective communication and advocacy with physicians and therapists, schools, and others involved in care and support for children with PANDAS or PANS.

What does it mean to be an advocate?

Wolfensberger (1973) defined advocacy as:

> speaking, acting, [or] writing with minimum conflict of interest on behalf of the sincerely perceived interests of a person or group, in order to promote, protect or defend the welfare of, and justice for, either individuals or groups, in a fashion which strives to be emphatic and vigorous. (Wolfensberger quoted in Cocks and Duffy 1993, p.41)

If we consider this definition section by section, we can see that advocates—including parent advocates—might accomplish several essential tasks on behalf of their children. Parent advocates speak (or write) for their children and perform actions on their behalf when appropriate. Furthermore, they do this in the best interests of their child, not their own interest. The goal of all of this activity is to "protect" their well-being or secure "justice" for their child. And advocacy is both "emphatic" and "vigorous," leaving no doubt about the fact that parent advocates sometimes need to ruffle feathers to articulate and secure the best interests of their children.

Importance of communicating

In practical terms, advocacy—focused communication on behalf of one's child (or other individual) with PANDAS or PANS—is essential in a multitude of spheres. Particularly because awareness of PANDAS, PANS, and related conditions continues to evolve, parents and family members play a critical role in communicating about the conditions themselves, their impact on children's daily living and functioning, and appropriate modalities for treatment. Effective advocacy requires parents to be well informed (Foster, Rude, and Grannan 2012) and, sometimes, persistent.

Becoming an advocate

Becoming an advocate for your child is not an overnight process, and that process may not follow a linear trajectory. While research has found parents typically experience empowerment and satisfaction with successful advocacy (Conley Wright and Taylor 2014), their journey to becoming an advocate may occur gradually, as they become more comfortable with the role of parent and as they (or their children) encounter different challenges. One's spheres of activity may change as well. For example, Mindy, a parent of three children with PANDAS, stepped into advocating for broader policy changes only after her children were stable, focusing first on securing their medical well-being through individual advocacy with their primary care provider.

Self-care while advocating for your child

Parenting a child with medical, behavioral, emotional, and/or academic needs can be taxing for caregivers. Particularly if advocacy involves conflict, it may be even more draining than your regular caregiving activities. Research has found, in fact, that some parents report feeling tired by the need to advocate for their children so often. Prioritize self-care for yourself to the degree that you can. This may involve letting another activity or commitment go, releasing yourself from guilt over unaccomplished tasks, or trading weekend mornings with your partner so that each of you can have a turn sleeping in and resting. It may also involve seeking respite care if available, so that you (and/or your partner) can have a few hours to rest or regroup.

Specific situations
Healthcare providers (including both medical providers and therapists)

In advocating for your child's needs with care providers, you will save a great deal of effort by choosing, when possible, a provider who is already familiar with PANDAS or PANS. If your healthcare provider is not familiar with PANDAS and PANS, expect to spend some time educating him or her. You might make it a habit to send abstracts of new peer-reviewed journal articles as they are published, increasing his or her knowledge of the evidence base underlying PANDAS and PANS treatment. When requesting an unusual test or treatment (for example, requesting a strep test solely on the basis of unusual behavior in your child), be polite but persistent, and, again, cite medical research whenever possible. Local parent groups, which can often be located on social media, can be excellent sources of support and suggestions for advocating with healthcare providers, and most PANDAS or PANS parents are more than willing to share information about articles, research, and approaches they have found helpful.

Schools

Other chapters address the role of communication and service coordination in school settings. Advocacy is another important dimension of coordinating an effective service plan. In our experience, the best way to advocate for your child with school personnel is to share your story openly. Request a meeting prior to your "official" IEP or 504 plan meeting at which you can share photos of your child and stories of his or her behavior before and after symptom onset. Throughout your interactions with school personnel, continue to remind the staff with whom you're working that your child is an individual who has a significant neurological illness. It is helpful, also, to consider pros and cons of escalating concerns. There may be times when you feel your child's needs are not being adequately addressed at the school level. In such cases, one option is to escalate the concern to the district, state, or federal (including civil rights monitoring) level. You may find that it is useful to bring a complaint to the school district; if your child has an IEP or 504 plan, you may also explore options for bringing a due process complaint and going through the legal process specified under each law. That being said, escalation may come at a significant cost in terms of relationships with school personnel. You can minimize this impact by being polite, professional, and personally appreciative for their efforts, despite your substantive disagreements. You may also reach a point where you feel the relationship has deteriorated to the point where your child's success or well-being will be jeopardized in either case. No matter what, under no circumstances should you let concerns about animosity or controversy dissuade you from advocating for your child when you truly believe his or her legal rights are in jeopardy.

Clergy and places of worship

Individuals with disabilities may encounter barriers in faith settings, including religious education (Carter 2007). Advocacy in this context may mean educating members (and leaders) of your faith community about your child's sensory and physical needs; it may mean suggesting key modifications that would facilitate your child's participation in faith-related activities. Carter (2007) identifies multiple areas in which faith communities should integrate individuals with disabilities, ranging from physical accessibility to religious education programming. The following questions, based in part on that framework, offer a starting place for family members in considering how accessible their faith community is and how to open conversations with community leaders about furthering their child's ability to participate in faith-based activities (see Box 15.1).

Box 15.1: Is my place of worship accessible for my child with PANDAS or PANS?

The following questions may help to guide families in anticipating potential needs their child may have while participating in worship activities and may help to guide conversations with clergy or other leaders of the faith community in ensuring greater accessibility.

- Is there seating readily available in case my child becomes dizzy or faint?

- Are there areas appropriate for a sensory break (dim side rooms, quiet vestibule areas, etc.)? Are those areas easy to get to when needed?

- Is the routine predictable so that my child and I can anticipate and plan for any elements of the service that could pose sensory or behavioral challenges?

- Is seating structured so that my child can participate in the service without being in close proximity to others during cold and flu season?

- Is there hand sanitizer available at entrances and exits?

- Is programming (religious education, Vacation Bible School, Hebrew School, youth group, etc.) modified for students who need specific changes or modifications?

- Have clergy and other personnel been trained on specific needs of children with PANDAS/PANS, chronic health needs, and neurological or immune conditions?

Individuals in the community

When advocating for your child in the community, you may vary the type and amount of information you provide based on:

- the situation

- the role of the person involved and their need for information

- the amount of time they will spend interacting with your child, and

- the degree of privacy afforded for your interactions.

For example, you may let your child's community league basketball coach know about her diagnosis in order to ensure she gets appropriate breaks for rest or anxiety management; at the mall, if your child is experiencing distress, it may be more appropriate simply to let a store clerk know she does not like to be touched, does not want to try clothes on, or whatever the specific issue is. You may already make decisions about community advocating on the go without realizing it or making it explicit.

Conclusion and key points

As parents and caregivers, it is natural to want the best for our children and to take steps to secure it as much as we can. Advocacy in pursuit of these goals is often a learned skill, one that we can develop if it does not come naturally. Advocacy can involve communicating with medical providers, schools, community members, and other individuals to educate them about your child's condition and share specific needs your child may have as well as specific strategies to support them.

In advocating, remember to:

- *Be assertive*: Don't be afraid to ask for what you know your child needs and to articulate why he or she needs it.

- *Remain polite*: Efforts at advocating for your child are far more likely to be successful when grounded in courtesy and strong existing relationships.

- *Escalate when necessary*: Particularly when your child's legal rights are at stake, be willing to share concerns with higher authorities and request relief from appropriate channels, including legal ones when truly necessary.

16

School Supports, Accommodations, and Adaptations

Rhonda felt overwhelmed heading into a meeting with her son's teachers. Garrett had been diagnosed with PANS three months before, had spent the last two and a half months out of school receiving treatment, and was now returning to fourth grade. Garrett's teachers had known nothing about PANS prior to his diagnosis, and his gym teacher, in particular, had been very reluctant to excuse his absences and his non-participation when his obsessive-compulsive symptoms flared up. The night before the meeting, Rhonda sat down with the handout she had found on various websites and made a master list of accommodations and supports that she thought might be helpful to Garrett. They included flexibility in attendance; extra time; a "flash pass" to go to the restroom, the nurse's office, or the guidance counselor; additional one-on-one help in math to help him get back on track; and a specialized behavior plan so that he would not "get in trouble" when experiencing tics or OCD symptoms. Looking at her list, Rhonda took a deep breath. "I hope they're on board with all of this!" she whispered to herself.

PANDAS and PANS often have a substantial impact on a student's ability to attend school (Rice Doran and O'Hanlon 2015), so for some families in acute crisis, school accommodations and supports may fall by the wayside as more urgent issues are addressed. At some point, however, many children return to school or seek to return to full functioning within their school environment, and at that point, school accommodations and supports become quite important.

Accommodations and supports for children with PANDAS/PANS who attend school are addressed more comprehensively in other resources, including the books *PANDAS and PANS in School Settings: A Handbook for Educators* (Rice Doran 2016) and *PANS, CANS and Automobiles: A Comprehensive Reference for Helping Students with PANDAS and PANS* (Candelaria-Greene 2016). This chapter provides a brief overview of considerations in selecting and implementing school accommodations, modifications or adaptations, and general supports, with the understanding that more detailed information can be found in these additional resources.

Background and importance of school supports

In the United States, equal access to education is guaranteed to all qualifying students with disabilities through Section 504 of the Rehabilitation Act of 1973 (34 CFR, Part 104.4). Additionally, the Individuals with Disabilities Education Act of 1990 (IDEA), reauthorized as the Individuals with Disabilities Education Improvement Act (IDEIA) of 2004, guarantees a free and appropriate public education (FAPE) to all students with an educational disability, including related services, accommodations, and IEPs when needed. In general, the threshold to qualify for accommodations under Section 504 is lower than the threshold to qualify for services and modifications under IDEIA, though each student's case is treated on an individual basis according to his or her unique needs. There is a specific process for determining whether a student has a disability and what its specific impact might be. This process may look slightly different from state to state but will have some key elements in common, such as the use of multiple sources of data and involvement of team members from multiple disciplines.

In general, there are important distinctions between the types of changes or forms of flexibility available to students (and their families) under these laws. Students may receive accommodations, which provide equal access and remove barriers imposed by disability while allowing students to meet the same curriculum demands as those without disabilities. They may also receive program modifications, which change the curriculum demands and material and generally are provided under IDEIA. As part of an IEP or 504 plan, students may also receive related services such as speech therapy, occupational therapy, counseling services, or physical therapy. Sometimes, school personnel may refer generally to "supports," which is a more general term that encompasses instructional materials, teaching techniques, or access to additional staff and services. "Supports" may refer to items provided under a 504 plan, an IEP, or both. At times, teams may provide some informal classroom supports on a short-term basis even before a student is formally identified as having a disability. And finally, some schools may provide specialized health plans that spell out health-related adaptations, such as flexible attendance or special cleaning protocols, related to the student's medical needs.

Symptoms and school impact

Whether a child is eligible for assistance under Section 504, IDEIA, or a stand-alone health plan, those involved in the planning process should begin by making a list of frequent or disruptive symptoms and their manifestations at school. This list can drive selection of accommodations or supports; it can also help to educate school personnel, who may not have seen all these symptoms connected previously. A sample list is presented in Table 16.1. Table 16.2 presents a template that can be used to generate a list.

Table 16.1: Sample list of symptoms and impact in school

Child's name	
Symptom	**Impact in school**
Obsessive-compulsive symptoms	Needs to use "correct" color pen
Sleep issues	Cannot walk down hall if there is paper crumpled up on floor
Urinary issues	Arrives at school very tired 50% of time
Handwriting difficulties	Needs a "flash pass" to use restroom
Oppositional behavior	Must use netbook or laptop
	May refuse with strong language if asked to do something that triggers anxiety or OCD; benefits from positive and gentle approach with time to respond, rather than direct commands

Table 16.2: Template for sample list

Child's name	
Symptom	**Impact in school**

Common accommodations

In one recent study, parents reported that students often utilized extended time, flexible attendance, and flexibility in homework (Rice Doran and O'Hanlon 2015). Parents also reported that students benefit from behavioral supports such as "safe places" to go in school when symptoms escalate and positive reinforcements rather than negative consequences for undesired behaviors (Rice Doran and O'Hanlon 2015). Use of technology, such as notetaking pens, recording devices for lectures, and laptops, can be extremely helpful for students with motor and processing difficulties, deficits which are often associated with PANDAS exacerbations (Calaprice *et al.* 2017a; Murphy *et al.* 2012).

Common modifications

The term "accommodations" generally refers to a school's ability to provide adjustments in the presentation, setting, timing, and response modality that students use in class and on assessments. The term "modifications," in contrast, refers to changes (usually reductions) in expectations for workload, curriculum, or content mastery. For example, a student may receive an audio version of a book as an accommodation for reading challenges; teachers might also opt to provide a modification of expectations by shortening the length of assigned reading. Most often, students receiving modified curriculum will be served with an IEP, as modifications are generally considered beyond the scope of a 504 plan or an informal support plan.

Students with PANDAS and PANS may exhibit diminished capacity for self-regulation, executive functioning, and timely processing. For these reasons, they may benefit in particular from reduced workload and shortened assignments across multiple content areas. Additionally, students with PANDAS or PANS may benefit from curriculum-specific modifications in certain subject areas: being excused from foreign language or math for a specific period of time, for example.

Other common supports

Some additional supports may not be formalized at the level required for an IEP or 504 plan; however, teachers often find themselves implementing informal, additional supports for students who need them. Such flexibility, in fact, is a fundamental part of differentiated instruction and best practice for inclusion. These supports may include checking in with students frequently; providing advance warning of transitions or changes in plans; reviewing or reinforcing directions one-on-one; and individualized behavior incentive systems. Any of these can be written into a formal plan; however, if students are typically functioning at a high enough level that these are the only supports they require, teachers and parents may elect to simply monitor the student's progress and adjust as needed.

Attendance strategies

For children with PANDAS or PANS, attendance is often a challenging topic meriting its own discussion. The combination of health needs, separation anxiety, and generalized phobia can create powerful barriers to a child's regular school attendance. Described below are some of the most common challenges students may experience with attendance, along with strategies to mitigate their impact or productively collaborate and communicate with school personnel regarding the issues.

Health considerations

Students with a PANDAS or PANS diagnosis are at risk for lowered immunity and greater sensitivity to infection or illness. Additionally, due to the multidisciplinary nature of PANDAS and PANS care, they often have multiple appointments with healthcare providers for office visits and procedures. Students receiving IVIG or plasmapheresis may need to miss school for days at a time; some parents and providers may opt to have students stay home if airborne vaccines, such as FluMist, are administered or during periods when illnesses seem to be circulating in greater numbers (such as cold or flu season). All of these considerations can cause significant disruptions in student attendance. Strategies to address this include:

- *Assemble relevant medical documentation and share with school personnel*: If you anticipate your child will need to miss school following IVIG administration, or you have dates for physician appointments, communicate with the school nurse or attendance office in advance. If your child needs a provider note for extended absence (such as hospitalization for plasmapheresis), obtain the note and provide it when you discuss the absence.

- *Know the options available to your child*: Different districts and states have different policies for home instruction, concurrent home and school teaching, or hospital-based teaching. Research your district's policy and obtain a clear picture of the options available for you and your child. Recognize that the best option for your child may change based on his or her changing medical needs, and remind school personnel of that fact as well.

- *Communicate and plan proactively with teachers*: Especially for extended absences, work with teachers to ensure they are aware of your child's status and can provide schoolwork as needed. If your child's medical needs are too intense to warrant completing work while out of school (for example, if your child will be undergoing a taxing procedure), share that fact as well so that your child's teachers can allow an adequate timeframe for makeup work.

Separation anxiety and generalized anxiety or phobias

These disorders are discussed in detail in preceding chapters; however, a brief discussion here focuses on management of anxiety at school, as these symptoms are often cited as being particularly disruptive in a school setting. Separation anxiety is an acute symptom of PANDAS and PANS and considered a "hallmark" of the disorder (Kovacevic n.d.). Separation anxiety, in particular, may make it difficult for students with PANDAS or PANS to leave home or leave a preferred parent to attend school, especially for a full day. Children with PANDAS or PANS often also exhibit generalized anxiety, which (as in children without PANDAS/PANS) can interfere with their availability to focus in school or their willingness to attend. Last, the obsessive-compulsive nature of PANDAS or PANS symptoms can lead some students to develop specific phobias that may be attached to objects, people, or experiences at school. For example, a student might have a phobia of public restrooms and be unable to attend school for a full day because it would require using a school restroom. A student might have an obsessive need to avoid the color green and may experience distress because the school's front doors are green. Strategies for addressing these issues are outlined in Chapters 9 and 10 as well.

Consult with your medical team to ensure your child is truly well enough to attend

Intense PANDAS or PANS symptoms, including severe separation anxiety or phobias, often are indicative of serious illness. If your child's separation anxiety has returned with a vengeance in the last two weeks, start by consulting with your provider to rule out new infections or complications with immune functioning. School refusal, or reluctance to attend, may be a symptom of significant physical illness and should be evaluated as such with the support of a knowledgeable healthcare provider.

Identify the underlying issue

Is your child unwilling or unable to attend school because of his attachment to you? Her fear of leaving her bedroom? Her fear of loud noises? Each of these may require a different strategy to address, so it is important to determine exactly which issue presents the barrier. If you are working with a therapist or mental health clinician, that individual may be able to help you identify the issue and explore some potential strategies to address it.

Communicate with school staff

As for medical appointments and other medical absences, it is important that school staff understand that absences due to separation anxiety (or other anxieties) are also physically driven and not the result of a conscious choice to "skip school" or malinger. Getting this point across may require persistence and continued advocacy, as school staff who lack prior experience with PANDAS and PANS may view chronic absence through the lens of truancy and poor choice rather than through the lens of medical necessity.

Strategize appropriately, based on the nature of the concern

Your child's therapist and teacher may both have ideas about how to address specific concerns your child has. If he or she is worried about separating from you in the morning, a customized and consistent drop-off routine may help; if he or she has fear of the large green doors at the entrance, it may be appropriate to bring him or her in through another door. If you know the specific trigger that is causing concern to your child, share as much information as you can with school staff and invite them to collaborate in forming solutions.

Accept incremental progress and advocate for your school partners to do the same

For a child with significant separation anxiety, attending school for one hour a day during a flare may be a major accomplishment. With your child's therapist and medical team, determine how much school attendance is reasonable to expect, and share those expectations—and appropriate documentation—with school staff. For school staff who are used to seeing anxiety and school attendance solely through the paradigm of behavioral choice, this may take extended discussion, education, and advocacy.

Involve your child in creating a strategy

Often, children have a clear sense of what might actually work with them. Open a discussion with your child about under what circumstances they might feel comfortable returning to school. You might consider framing the question as, "What would school need to be like for you to feel comfortable there?" If school staff are willing to dialogue, you can share your child's answers with them and engage in shared planning. A special treat at drop-off, a "flash pass" to leave the classroom if it becomes overwhelming, or an option for a shortened day may make school more tolerable.

Conclusion and key points

Ensuring your child has access to needed supports in school, like other aspects of parenting a child with PANDAS or PANS, can be a complex process. Understanding the difference between various types of plans and school supports (including IEPs as well as concepts like accommodations, modifications, and other informal supports) may help you to be a more effective advocate. In addition, being well versed in your child's rights can be helpful; many large cities or states have parent information networks whose sole mission is to support parents of children with disabilities, and some of these may provide legal advice insofar as they are able. Last, planning for specific areas of difficulty, whether academic, behavioral, or attendance-related, is also helpful. Be mindful of the following, in particular:

— Be aware of your child's rights and do not be afraid to advocate, politely but firmly, for them.

— Consider how you define progress, and reward incremental improvements (completing an entire academic task, making it through a half day) as they occur.

— Educate school personnel about PANDAS and PANS in general and specific areas of need, such as OCD and attendance challenges, in particular.

17

Guidance for Clinicians

WHAT TO LOOK FOR AND HOW TO HELP

You may be wondering why a book designed for parents includes a chapter aimed at clinicians. Often, we have found that clinicians, particularly those in the mental health field, fall into one of two categories. Either they are quite familiar with PANDAS and PANS, to the point that they may be the ones to suggest parents pursue a PANDAS or PANS diagnosis with an appropriate physician, or, alternatively, they may have quite limited knowledge of both conditions. In this case, parents often end up educating their child's therapist, psychologist, or psychiatrist even as they educate themselves. For this reason, we provide some general suggestions for clinicians, which may be useful both to mental health professionals reading this book and to parents sharing and passing along information.

Collected clinical, research, and anecdotal evidence shows that a missed PANDAS/PANS diagnosis has resulted in many children being placed on unnecessary psychiatric medications or in more restrictive costly psychiatric facilities, possibly causing more harm than healing. Tragically, multiple children have been so overcome by the suffering that they turned to suicide. Mental health clinicians of all domains can help by being informed about PANDAS/PANS and able to recognize the symptoms. This knowledge involves being able to connect the client's medical history with the sudden onset of neuropsychiatric symptoms. Clinicians can have a very important role with this disorder by recognizing sudden onset and assisting with differential diagnosis. This may include helping to rule out pre-existing mental health issues, trauma or abuse, significant life changes, toxins, substance abuse, or other medical/neurological conditions as reasons for the current abrupt changes in the child. Remember to refer for required medical exams/laboratory workups as needed, or to suggest to parents that they seek that testing from another professional if it lies outside your expertise to recommend or order it.

Even though PANDAS/PANS is a medical and neurological condition, mental health clinicians can have great impact by being aware of and able to distinguish PANDAS symptoms from other mental health disorders and guide these suffering children to the correct treatment arena. Many clinicians have found the published diagnosis and treatment guidelines (see the *Journal of Child and Adolescent Psychopharmacology*, February 2015 and September 2017), as well as published research found on the PANDAS Network[1] and PANDAS Physician Network[2] websites, to be helpful for guidance.

It is very important to believe and validate the parent and child's experience with PANDAS/PANS. Families find it terrifying, at times, to have these unusual symptoms suddenly occur with their child and to be at a complete loss to know what it is or how to treat it. Additional stress is added if the parent has the experience of having their concerns minimized, dismissed, or rejected by the very medical community they turn to for help. Informed parents know their children and yet are often not able to convince doctors to acknowledge or treat PANDAS/PANS. Clinicians can advocate for the client's needs with physicians, schools, and in the community by having the research and resources ready to assist in combating any barriers blocking the child's treatment. Understand that the family is in crisis and help by providing education to shocked parents and alerting them to the need for quick medical interventions for best treatment outcome. Help families understand the clinical course of PANDAS, including the unpredictable episodic pattern, and help to translate pertinent reliable research information for parents and provide established professional resources and treatment guidance.

Identify supports for parents, both formal and informal, and link families with local PANDAS/PANS advocacy and support groups. The burden of this disorder is great and parents are extremely stressed, often feeling isolated and living in constant fear of symptom relapse in their child. Clinicians can provide a sense of hope and much-needed

1   www.pandasnetwork.org
2   www.pandasppn.org

emotional support. Assist to coordinate treatment referrals to PANDAS/PANS-knowledgeable physicians and specialists (see the PANDAS Network website for lists by state). Collaborate with, and often inform, multidisciplinary treatment providers to address both the medical and mental health symptoms. Assist families with seeking insurance coverage or financial resources for the more expensive medical interventions. There is something uniquely shocking about a sudden and profound psychiatric change in a child. Arrange for aftercare if PTSD sets in, as parents can often be traumatized by the experience of their child suddenly being very ill and the lengthy course of seeking answers and proper medical care.

Assess the child on a symptom severity scale and use the published PANDAS/PANS treatment guidelines to plan interventions or to refer to medical providers who can (depending on your specific field of expertise). Help the overwhelmed parents to track all symptoms and treatment interventions, and assess outcomes. Be aware that medical treatment alone may alleviate many symptoms, but therapy is still useful with residual issues and any future flares the client may experience. Cognitive behavioral therapy (CBT) may be the most effective therapy approach in PANDAS/PANS thus far. During the acute phase of illness, the child may not be ready to fully participate in sessions; however, it is helpful when parents receive support and learn coping strategies so that they can support implementation when their child is ready.

Work with parents to set clear limits and consequences, positively reinforce desired behaviors with their child, and establish reward systems. Teach parents to remain calm and be grounding for their child, and help them to manage their own fear and stress and not to release it on the child. Help parents to model self-regulation, so the child can learn how to manage their own anxiety. Work with parents to be on the same page with parenting and to discipline the illness symptoms, not the child. Parenting a special needs child often involves loss, grief, and the acceptance of a new normal, thus teaching self-care skills to families is vital. Initiate CBT with the child once they are stable, with the goal of avoiding establishing negative behavior patterns. Interventions can include encouraging the child to identify triggers using the antecedent–behavior–consequence (ABC) model, exposure and response prevention, thought replacement, practicing relaxation and de-escalation strategies, habit reversal training, and rewarding brave behaviors. This is not a typical behavior disorder, but a brain disease, so clinicians need to be creative in order to make traditional interventions effective.

Provide psychoeducation on the disorder and help the child to understand the involved brain response and gently begin to confront their anxiety. Separation anxiety with PANDAS/PANS frequently interferes with normal family functioning, restricting both the child's and the parents' activities. Reassure parents that short-term accommodation of the anxiety may be tolerable if medical interventions are working. During the acute illness phase, modifying activities and minimizing transitions may be needed, but the child should return to a normal daily routine as soon as possible. Encourage families to avoid long-term accommodation of the child's anxieties to prevent reinforcing new rituals. Remember, the child is not in control of this behavioral disruption, so parents need to choose the battles worth fighting. As with the treatment of all mental health issues, creating safety is critical, so frequently assess and address any self-harm threats or behaviors and develop an emergency plan with the family.

Key points

- Know the symptoms and change the outcome. PANDAS is not rare; it is simply rarely diagnosed correctly (Westly 2009).

- PANDAS/PANS is treatable, but early identification and correct treatment results in a more successful outcome.

- Treatment takes a multidisciplinary team approach, with coordinated medical and mental health services.

Action steps for clinicians

- Automatically consider PANDAS/PANS if there is a sudden change from the baseline of functioning and an acute onset of psychiatric symptoms in a child. Refer to physicians for necessary exams and labs and assist with differential diagnosis.

- Validate, support, and advocate for parents with doctors and schools, and in the community.

- Increase awareness and share PANDAS/PANS knowledge with any pediatric professionals.

18

Conclusion

In conceptualizing, drafting, and revising this manuscript, we have often felt as though we were sitting at a coffee table giving advice to a friend navigating this difficult world of PANDAS and PANS. Indeed, while we will not know every parent or caregiver who picks up this book, we do feel in some sense as though we are friends, united by the intense bond of navigating, and surviving, this intense and sometimes debilitating illness. As we have stated in prior chapters, none of us would elect to join the PANDAS or PANS community but, once in it, we can certainly appreciate the caring and fellowship that characterizes it.

Several chapters have addressed specific strategies for certain areas of PANDAS or PANS symptoms or provided practical guidance to resolve specific problems, such as disruptive OCD or the need to explain PANDAS to teachers. Other chapters have explored difficult but common issues, such as family trauma and relationship strain. Some of these, you may notice, are written in a more conversational or reflective vein, and this also is intentional; some of these topics lend themselves to moral support and affirmation as well as research-based exploration. Our experience as family members, as well as professionals, has taught us that both are essential in helping families to continue to thrive while dealing with this challenging diagnosis.

In future years, we hope, many of the complications explored in this book, such as relationship strain and child suicide, will have grown to be rare, all but eradicated by increased awareness, early detection, and effective, widely available treatment. Until then, we hope increased advocacy by our determined parent and family community can help to close the gap, providing parents with much-needed advice, information, and (most essential of all) support.

Appendix

PANS Family Safety Plan

Child's name:
Diagnosis:
Birthdate: Age:
Triggers
Techniques for de-escalation
Instructions for other family members during time of crisis
Family/friend support contact information
Medication list and dosages

Physician contact information

Other health professional contact information

Crisis services

Police non-emergency phone number

Other information

References

Adrion, E.R., Aucott, J., Lemke, K.W., and Weiner, J.P. (2015) "Health care costs, utilization and patterns of care following Lyme Disease." *PLoS ONE 10*, 2, e0116767.

Allen, A., Leonard, H., and Swedo, S. (1995) "Case study: a new infection-triggered, autoimmune subtype of pediatric OCD and Tourette's syndrome." *Journal of the American Academy of Child and Adolescent Psychiatry 34*, 307–311.

American Psychiatric Association (2007) *Practice Guideline for the Treatment of Patients with Obsessive-Compulsive Disorder.* Arlington, VA: American Psychiatric Association. Accessed on Oct. 20, 2018 at https://psychiatryonline.org/pb/assets/raw/sitewide/practice_guidelines/guidelines/ocd.pdf

Anxiety and Depression Association of America (ADAA) (n.d.) "Generalized Anxiety Disorder." Accessed on Oct. 1, 2018 at https://adaa.org/understanding-anxiety/generalized-anxiety-disorder-gad#

Brown, B. (2017) *Rising Strong: How the Ability to Reset Transforms the Way we Live, Love, Parent and Lead.* New York: Random House.

Brown, K.D., Farmer, C., Freeman, G.M., Spartz, E.J., *et al.* (2017) "Effect of early and prophylactic nonsteroidal anti-inflammatory drugs on flare duration in pediatric acute-onset neuropsychiatric syndrome: an observational study of patients followed by an academic community-based pediatric acute-onset neuropsychiatric syndrome clinic." *Journal of Child and Adolescent Psychopharmacology 27*, 7, 619-628.

Cahalan, S. (2012) *Brain on Fire: My Month of Madness.* New York: Simon and Schuster.

Calaprice, D., Tona, J., and Murphy, T.K. (2017a) "Treatment of pediatric acute-onset neuropsychiatric disorder in a large survey population." *Journal of Child and Adolescent Psychopharmacology*, August, doi: https://doi.org/10.1089/cap.2017.0101

Calaprice, D., Tona, J., Parker-Athill, E.C., and Murphy, T.K. (2017b) "A survey of pediatric acute onset neuropsychiatric syndrome characteristics and course." *Journal of Child and Adolescent Psychopharmacology 27*, 7, 607–618.

Candelaria-Greene, J. (2016) *PANS, CANS and Automobiles: A Comprehensive Reference Guide for Helping Students with PANDAS and PANS.* Sarasota, FL: First Edition Design Publishing.

Carter, E. (2007) *Including People with Disabilities in Faith Communities*, 1st edn. Baltimore, MD: Brookes Publishing.

Case Management Society of America (n.d.) "What Is a Case Manager?" Accessed on Oct. 15, 2018 at www.cmsa.org/who-we-are/what-is-a-case-manager

Celik, G., Tas, D., Tahiroglu, A., Avci, A., Yuksel, B., and Cam, P. (2016) "Vitamin D deficiency in obsessive-compulsive disorder patients with pediatric autoimmune neuropsychiatric disorders associated with streptococcal infections: a case control study." *Nöro Psikiyatri Arşivi 53*, 1, 33–37.

Chang, K., Frankovich, J., Cooperstock, M., Cunningham, M.W., *et al.* (2015) "Clinical evaluation of youth with pediatric acute-onset neuropsychiatric syndrome (PANS): recommendations from the 2013 PANS Consensus Conference." *Journal of Child and Adolescent Psychopharmacology 25*, 1, 3–13.

Church, A., Cardoso, G., Dale, R., Lees, A, Thompson, E., and Giovannoni, G. (2002) "Anti-basal ganglia antibodies in acute and persistent Sydenham's chorea." *Neurology 59*, 2, 227–231.

Cocks, E. and Duffy, G. (1993) *The Nature and Purposes of Advocacy for People with Disabilities*. Perth, Australia: Edith Cowan University. Accessed on Dec. 10, 2018 at https://ro.ecu.edu.au/ecuworks/7172

Conley Wright, A. and Taylor, S. (2014) "Advocacy by parents of young children with special needs: activities, processes, and perceived effectiveness." *Journal of Social Service Research 40*, 5, 591–605.

Connery, K., Tippett, M., Delhey, L.M., Rose, S., *et al.* (2018) "Intravenous immunoglobulin for the treatment of autoimmune encephalopathy in children with autism." *Translational Psychiatry 8*, 148, http://doi.org/10.1038/s41398-018-0214-7

Cooperstock, M.S., Swedo, S.E., Pasternack, M.S., and Murphy, T.K. (2017) "Clinical management of pediatric acute-onset neuropsychiatric syndrome: Part III—Treatment and prevention of infections." *Journal of Child and Adolescent Psychopharmacology 27*, 7, 594–606.

Copeland, M.E. (2018) "Wellness Recovery Action Plan." Accessed on Sept. 29, 2018 at http://mentalhealthrecovery.com/wrap-is

Cunningham-Rundles, C. (2011) "Autoimmunity in primary immune deficiency: taking lessons from our patients." *Clinical and Experimental Immunology 164*, Suppl. 2, 6–11.

Dalmau, J. and Graus, G. (2018) "Antibody-mediated encephalitis." *New England Journal of Medicine 378*, 9, 840–851.

Davidsson, M. (2018) "The financial implications of a well-hidden and ignored chronic Lyme disease pandemic." *Healthcare 6*, 1, 16.

Farmer, C., Thienemann, M., Leibold, C., Kamalani, G., Sauls, B., and Frankovich, J. (2018) "Psychometric evaluation of the Caregiver Burden Inventory in children and adolescents with PANS." *Journal of Pediatric Psychology 43*, 7, 749–757.

Flegr, J. (2013) "Influence of latent *toxoplasma* infection on human personality, physiology and morphology: pros and cons of the *toxoplasma*–human model in studying the manipulation hypothesis." *Journal of Experimental Biology 216*, 127–133.

Foster, A., Rude, D., and Grannan, C. (2012) "Preparing parents to advocate for a child with autism." *Phi Delta Kappan 94*, 4, 16–20.

Frankovich, J., Swedo, S., Murphy, T., Dale, R.C., *et al.* (2017) "Clinical management of pediatric acute-onset neuropsychiatric syndrome: Part II—Use of immunomodulatory therapies." *Journal of Child and Adolescent Psychopharmacology 27*, 7, 574–593.

Garland, E.M., Celedonio, J.E., and Raj, S.R. (2015) "Postural tachycardia syndrome: beyond orthostatic intolerance." *Current Neurology and Neuroscience Reports 15*, 9, 60.

Gaughan, T., Buckley, A., Hommer, R., Grant, P., *et al.* (2016) "Rapid eye movement sleep abnormalities in children with pediatric acute-onset neuropsychiatric syndrome (PANS)." *Journal of Clinical Sleep Medicine 12*, 7, 1027–1032.

Harris, A. (2014) "PANDAS: A little-known disorder with a large impact." *The Irish Times* Oct. 14. Accessed on Dec. 10, 2018 at www.irishtimes.com/life-and-style/health-family/pandas-a-little-known-disorder-with-a-large-impact-1.1955088

Harvard Health (2018) "Understanding the Stress Response." Accessed on Oct. 1, 2018 at www.health.harvard.edu/staying-healthy/understanding-the-stress-response

Huppert, J.D. and Roth, D.A. (2003) "Treating obsessive-compulsive disorder with exposure and response prevention." *The Behavior Analyst Today 4*, 1, 66–70.

Individuals with Disabilities Education Improvement Act of 2004. Pub.L. 108–446, 20 U.S.C. §1400 et seq.

Insel, T. (2012) "From Paresis to PANDAS and PANS." National Institute of Mental Health. Accessed on Oct. 1, 2018 at www.nimh.nih.gov/about/directors/thomas-insel/blog/2012/from-paresis-to-pandas-and-pans.shtml

International OCD Foundation (n.d.) "About OCD." Accessed on Oct. 1, 2018 at https://iocdf.org/about-ocd

Journal of Child and Adolescent Psychopharmacology 25, 1 (2015) "Special issue on pediatric acute-onset neuropsychiatric syndrome."

Journal of Child and Adolescent Psychopharmacology 27, 1 (2017)

Khakpour, P. (2018) *Sick*. New York: Harper Collins.

Kovacevic, M. (n.d.) "PANDAS and PITAND Syndromes." *WebPediatrics.com* Accessed on Sept. 28, 2018 at www.webpediatrics.com/pandas.html

Kurlan, R., Johnson, D., Kaplan, E.L. and Tourette Syndrome Study Group (2008) "Streptococcal infection and exacerbations of childhood tics and obsessive-compulsive symptoms: a prospective blinded cohort study." *Pediatrics 121*, 6, 1188–1197.

Kushner, H. (2004) *When Bad Things Happen to Good People: 20th Anniversary Edition*. New York: Random House.

Lehmann, M.L., Weigel, T.K., Cooper, H.A., Elkahloun, A.G., Kigar, S.L., and Herkenham, M. (2018) "Decoding microglia responses to psychosocial stress reveals blood–brain barrier breakdown that may drive stress susceptibility." *Scientific Reports 8*, 11240.

Linehan Institute (n.d.) "What Is Dialectical Behavior Therapy (DBT)?" Accessed on Oct. 1, 2018 at https://behavioraltech.org/resources/faqs/dialectical-behavior-therapy-dbt

Martin, B. (2018) "In-Depth: Cognitive Behavioral Therapy." *Psych Central.* Accessed on Oct. 10, 2018 at https://psychcentral.com/lib/in-depth-cognitive-behavioral-therapy

McClelland, M., Crombez, M., Crombez, C., Wenz, C., *et al.* (2015) "Implications for advanced practice nurses when pediatric autoimmune neuropsychiatric disorders associated with streptococcal infections (PANDAS) is suspected: a qualitative study." *Journal of Pediatric Health Care 29*, 442–452.

McLeod, S. (2010) "What Is the Stress Response?" Accessed on Sept. 15, 2018 at www.simplypsychology.org/stress-biology.html

Moleculera Labs (2018) "The Cunningham Panel." Accessed on Oct. 1, 2018 at www.moleculeralabs.com/cunningham-panel-pandas-pans-testing

Murphy, T.K., Patel, P.D., McGuire, J.F., Kennel, A., *et al.* (2015) "Characterization of the pediatric acute-onset neuropsychiatric syndrome phenotype." *Journal of Child and Adolescent Psychopharmacology 25*, 1, 14–25.

Murphy, T., Storch, E., Lewin, A., Edge, P., and Goodman, W. (2012) "Clinical factors associated with pediatric autoimmune neuropsychiatric disorders associated with streptococcal infections." *Journal of Pediatrics 160*, 2, 314–319.

Najjar, S., Pearlman, D.M., Alper, K., Najjar, A., and Devinsky, O. (2013) "Neuroinflammation and psychiatric illness." *Journal of Neuroinflammation 10*, 43.

National Institutes of Mental Health (NIMH) (2016) "Post-Traumatic Stress Disorder." Accessed on Oct. 1, 2018 at www.nimh.nih.gov/health/topics/post-traumatic-stress-disorder-ptsd/index.shtml

National Institutes of Mental Health (NIMH) (n.d.) "Information About PANS/PANDAS." Accessed on Nov. 14, 2018 at www.nimh.nih.gov/labs-at-nimh/research-areas/clinics-and-labs/sbp/information-about-pans-pandas.shtml

PANDAS Network (2015) "About PANDAS, PANS, and AE." Accessed Dec. 17, 2018 at http://pandasnetwork.org/medical-information

PANDAS Network (2018) *PN 2018 State of Our Children Survey (A Precursor to the PN Patient Registry).* Accessed on Dec. 10, 2018 at http://pandasnetwork.org/wp-content/uploads/2018/10/PN-SOOC-SURVEY_2018.pdf

PANDAS Physicians Network (2018a) "PANS: PPN Diagnostic Guidelines." Accessed on Oct. 1, 2018 at www.pandasppn.org/ppn-pans-diagnostic-guidelines

PANDAS Physicians Network (2018b) "SSRIs." Accessed Oct. 1, 2018 www.pandasppn.org/ssris

PANDAS Physicians Network (2018c) "Intravenous Immunoglobulin ('IVIG')." Accessed on Oct. 1, 2018 at www.pandasppn.org/ivig

Pawela, C., Brunsdon, R., Williams, T., Porter, M., *et al.* (2017) "The neuropsychological profile of children with basal ganglia encephalitis: a case series." *Developmental Medicine and Child Neurology 59*, 4, 445–448.

Platt, M., Agalliu, D., and Cutforth, T. (2017) "Hello from the other side: how autoantibodies circumvent the blood–brain barrier in autoimmune encephalitis." *Frontiers in Immunology 8*, 442, https://doi.org/10.3389/fimmu.2017.00442

Rasmussen, C. (2013) *Second Firsts: Live, Laugh and Love Again.* Carlsbad, CA: Hay House.

Rehabilitation Act of 1973. Pub.L. 93–112, 29 U.S.C. §701 et seq.

Rice Doran, P. (ed.) (2016) *PANDAS and PANS in School Settings: A Handbook for Educators*. Philadelphia, PA: Jessica Kingsley Publishers.

Rice Doran, P. and O'Hanlon, E. (2015) "Families' experiences with PANDAS and related disorders." Poster session at the Council for Exceptional Children Annual Convention: San Diego, CA.

Right Response (2018) "Can You De-escalate Anyone, Anywhere, Anytime?" Accessed on Oct. 1, 2018 at http://rightresponse.org/de-escalation-skills

Rollin, J. (2015) "4 Things Not to Say to Someone with an Anxiety Disorder." *Psychology Today*. Accessed on Oct. 1, 2018 at www.psychologytoday.com/us/blog/mindful-musings/201510/4-things-not-say-someone-anxiety-disorder

Samartano, M. (2018) "The stress reaction cycle." Accessed on Dec. 10, 2018 at https://psychcentral.com/blog/the-stress-reaction-cycle

Singer, H., Loiselle, C., Lee, O., Garvey, M., and Grus, F. (2003) "Anti-basal ganglia antibody abnormalities in Sydenham chorea." *Journal of Neuroimmunology 136*, 1–2, 154–161.

Snider, L., Lougee, L., Slattery, M., Grant, P., and Swedo, S. (2005) "Antibiotic prophylaxis with azithromycin or penicillin for childhood-onset neuropsychiatric disorders." *Biological Psychiatry 57*, 7, 788–792.

Sorel, T. (2016) *My Kid Is Not Crazy*. Regents of the University of Florida. Video file. Accessed on Oct. 1, 2018 at www.mykidisnotcrazy.com

Stanford Children's Health (n.d.) "Separation Anxiety Disorder." Accessed on Oct. 1, 2018 at www.stanfordchildrens.org/en/topic/default?id=separation-anxiety-disorder-90-P02582

Storch, E.A., Bussing, R., Jacob, M.L., Nadeau, J.M., *et al.* (2015) "Frequency and correlates of suicidal ideation in pediatric obsessive-compulsive disorder." *Child Psychiatry and Human Development 46*, 1, 75–83.

Swedo, S., Leckman, J., and Rose, N. (2012) "From research subgroup to clinical syndrome: modifying the PANDAS criteria to describe PANS (pediatric acute-onset neuropsychiatric syndrome)." *Pediatrics and Therapeutics 2*, 113.

Swedo, S., Leonard, H., Garvey, M., Mittleman, B., *et al.* (1998) "Pediatric autoimmune neuropsychiatric disorders associated with streptococcal infections: clinical description of the first 50 cases." *American Journal of Psychiatry 155*, 264–271.

The Understood Team (n.d.) "Understanding Executive Functioning Issues." Accessed on Dec. 10, 2018 at www.understood.org/en/learning-attention-issues/child-learning-disabilities/executive-functioning-issues/understanding-executive-functioning-issues

Thienemann, M. (2016) "Medical Background of PANDAS and PANS." In P. Rice Doran (ed.) *PANDAS and PANS in School Settings: A Handbook for Educators*. Philadelphia, PA: Jessica Kingsley Publishers.

Thienemann, M., Murphy, T., Leckman, J., Shaw, R., *et al.* (2017) "Clinical management of pediatric acute-onset neuropsychiatric syndrome: Part I—psychiatric and behavioral interventions." *Journal of Child and Adolescent Psychopharmacology 27*, 7, 566–573.

University of Minnesota Libraries Publishing (2018) *Communication in the Real World: An Introduction to Communication Studies*. Adapted and produced by University of Minnesota Libraries Publishing from a work produced and distributed under a Creative Commons license (CC BY-NC-SA; details at https://open.lib.umn.edu/communication/front-matter/publisher-information). Accessed on Dec. 10, 2018 at https://open.lib.umn.edu/communication/chapter/4-1-principles-and-functions-of-nonverbal-communication

Walters Wright, L. (n.d.) "7 Ideas for Using Rewards and Consequences." Accessed on Oct. 3, 2018 at www.understood.org/en/learning-attention-issues/understanding-childs-challenges/simple-changes-at-home/7-ideas-for-using-rewards-and-consequences

Weinstock, L.B., Brook, J.B., Myers, T.L., and Goodman, B. (2018) "Successful treatment of postural orthostatic tachycardia and mast cell activation syndromes using naltrexone, immunoglobulin and antibiotic treatment." *BMJ Case Reports*, http://doi.org/10.1136/bcr-2017-221405

Westly, E. (2009) "From throat to mind: strep today, anxiety later?" *Scientific American* Jan. 5. Accessed on Dec. 10, 2018 at www.scientificamerican.com/article/from-throat-to-mind

Williams, L. (2017) "Ambiguous Grief: Grieving Someone Who Is Still Alive." Accessed on Dec. 10, 2018 at https://whatsyourgrief.com/ambiguous-grief-grieving-someone-who-is-still-alive

Further Reading

Websites

Children's Postinfectious Autoimmune Encephalopathy Center: https://peds.
arizona.edu/cpae
The Foundation for Children with Neuroimmune Disorders: www.neuroimmune.
org
International OCD Foundation: www.iocdf.org/pandas
National Institute of Mental Health (NIMH): www.nimh.nih.gov
PANDAS Network: www.pandasnetwork.org
PANDAS/PANS Advocacy and Support: www.pas.care
PANDAS Physicians Network: www.pandasppn.org
Pediatric Research and Advocacy Initiative: http://praikids.org

Books

Chapman, A.L., Gratz, K.L., and Linehan, M.M. (2015) *The Dialectical Behavior Therapy Skills Workbook for Anger: Using DBT, Mindfulness and Emotion Regulation Skills to Manage Anger.* Oakland, CA: New Harbinger.

Chapman, A.L., Gratz, K.L., Tull, M.T., and Keane, T. (2011) *The Dialectical Behavior Therapy Skills Workbook for Anxiety: Breaking Free from Worry, Panic, PTSD, and Other Anxiety Symptoms.* Oakland, CA: New Harbinger.

Gibbs, E. (2012) *A Child's Introduction to Understanding PANDAS.* Scotts Valley, CA: CreateSpace.

Greene, D.C. (2016) *PANS, CANS, and Automobiles: A Comprehensive Reference Guide for Helping Students with PANDAS and PANS.* Scotts Valley, CA: CreateSpace.

Hueber, D. and Matthews, B. (2006) *What to Do When You Worry Too Much.* Washington, DC: Magination Press.

Hueber, D. and Matthews, B. (2007) *What to Do When You Grumble Too Much.* Washington, DC: Magination Press.

Hueber, D. and Matthews, B. (2007) *What to Do When Your Brain Gets Stuck.* Washington, DC: Magination Press.

Hueber, D. and Matthews, B. (2007) *What to Do When Your Temper Flares.* Washington, DC: Magination Press.

Hueber, D. and Matthews, B. (2008) *What to Do When You Dread your Bed.* Washington, DC: Magination Press.

Maloney, B. (2010) *Saving Sammy: A Mother's Fight to Cure Her Son's OCD.* New York: Broadway Books.

Maloney, B. (2013) *Childhood Interrupted: The Complete Guide to PANDAS and PANS.* Scotts Valley, CA: CreateSpace.

Murphy, T.K., Kurlan, R., and Leckman, J. (2010a) "The immunobiology of Tourette's disorder, pediatric autoimmune neuropsychiatric disorders associated with streptococcus, and related disorders: a way forward." *Journal of Child and Adolescent Psychopharmacology 20,* 317–331.

Murphy, T.K., Storch, E.A., Turner, A., Reid, J.M., Tan, J., and Lewin, A.B. (2010b) "Maternal history of autoimmune disease in children presenting with tics and/ or obsessive-compulsive disorder." *Journal of Neuroimmunology 229,* 1–2, 243–247.

Rathus, J.H. and Miller, A.L (2014) *DBT® Skills Manual for Adolescents.* New York: Guilford.

Rice Doran, P (ed.) (2016) *PANDAS and PANS in School Settings: A Handbook for Educators.* Philadelphia, PA: Jessica Kingsley Publishers.

Van Dijk, S. (2011) *Don't Let Your Emotions Run Your Life for Teens.* Oakland, CA: New Harbinger.

Weiss, M. (2015) *In a Pickle over PANDAS.* Sarasota, FL: First Edition Design Publishing.

Index